IBP HANDBOOK No. 13

Productivity of Terrestrial Animals
principles and methods

K. PETRUSEWICZ
and
A. MACFADYEN

INTERNATIONAL BIOLOGICAL PROGRAMME

7 MARYLEBONE ROAD, LONDON, NW1

F. A. DAVIS COMPANY
PHILADELPHIA · PA

591. 5
P498p
148291

Printed in Great Britain

Contents

Contents

Foreword

During the last few years, there has developed a new awareness of the loss of environmental substance and quality which is occurring throughout the world. The land which supplies man with much of his sustenance, both physical and spiritual, has been seriously, and sometimes irrevocably, degraded by many of his past activities. Moreover, in many areas this degradation continues apace. It is all too clear that the traditional ways of using our heritage of natural resources no longer suffice and that the single-purpose effort, with its lack of concern for or understanding of the consequences, must be abandoned in favour of a more rational utilization based on recognition of the fact that the biosphere is a system and that, like all systems, actions on one component or process affect all other parts. This in turn calls for a better understanding of the functioning of natural systems, which can only be based on integrated, interdisciplinary programmes of research and development.

Unesco, as part of its commitment to education, science and culture, has from the beginning been closely involved in the question of man's relationship with his environment and the problems attendant upon his utilization of natural resources. The Organization's scientific activities in the last twenty years, for instance, have included such major research programmes as those on the Arid Zones and Humid Tropics, the establishment of the Intergovernmental Oceanographic Commission and the launching in 1965 of the International Hydrological Decade.

At the same time close collaboration with the scientific community has always been a feature of Unesco's science policy. This is well illustrated by the large number of joint activities being undertaken by Unesco and the International Biological Programme (IBP), be they symposia, consultant missions or training seminars. Increased co-operation is envisaged in the coming years as the life span of the Programme comes to a close and the long-term intergovernmental and interdisciplinary programme on 'Man and

the Biosphere', the plan of which I shall be submitting to the General Con-
ference of Unesco at its sixteenth session in 1970, becomes operational.

This volume, like others in the series of *International Biological Programme Handbooks*, describes methods which can be recommended to research workers. It should be stressed that these are not formally agreed methods, since a standardized methodology would not only prove impossible to compile, but would also be stultifying to science. But in any international co-operative effort a basic recommended methodology is needed in order to ensure comparability of results.

The subject of this handbook, the secondary productivity of terrestrial ecosystems, is one of great interest to Unesco, and I am happy to commend it as a worthy and important issue in the *IBP Handbook Series*. I am confident that it will help stimulate and guide research on terrestrial consumer populations, thus furthering our understanding of ecosystem processes and functioning and facilitating a better management and conservation of our precious heritage of natural resources.

RENÉ MAHEU
Director-General
March 1970   UNESCO

Preface

Under the aegis of the IBP, a working meeting on Principles and Methods of Secondary Productivity of Terrestrial Ecosystems was held at Jabłonna from the 30th of August to the 6th of September 1966. The meeting was invited by the Polish Academy of Sciences and the organization was due to Professor Petrusewicz and his staff in the Department of Terrestrial Ecology of the Institute of Ecology. It was attended by 66 members from 14 countries and 54 papers were read. These were published in "Secondary Productivity of Terrestrial Ecosystems" by the Polish Academy of Sciences, Institute of Ecology, and the International Biological Programme, Section PT, in Warsaw and Cracow in 1967.

A purpose of many technical meetings convened by IBP has been to advise on methods of research. The aim is not that of standardization—for ecological science is still evolving rapidly through the improvement of its methodology—but to give workers in different parts of the world a means whereby their results will be comparable with results by other workers in other areas. Therefore, after the Jabłonna meeting the authors were invited by Section PT (Productivity Terrestrial) of the IBP to collaborate in producing a handbook which should draw together into a convenient form the modern ideas and methods in this subject. We were given complete freedom as to how this should be done.

A brief of this kind presents difficulties: should, for instance, an attempt be made to survey all the topics of discussion in such a way as to reflect equally the views and contributions of the members of the meeting, or should the handbook authors feel themselves at liberty to write a more personal book in the hope that this would be better integrated? Should they be free to draw on material which was only slightly touched upon or even not mentioned at the meeting?

We decided on the latter course because we felt that (1) there was a considerable degree of duplication and some corresponding omissions in the original material of the meeting; and (2) as a result of extensive and often lively discussions and an unusually successful exercise in mutual education at the meeting, many of us—the authors included—experienced considerable changes in views and emphasis. It would now be pointless to revert to a system of thought which has become historical and is already fully documented in the reports of the proceedings.

The handbook which follows, then, is a personal document for which we must take full responsibility. It has not always been easy to agree on what to say or how to say it. Our discussions have been many and prolonged and the final outcome has usually been based, we believe, on understanding rather than on compromise. Some participants at the Jabłonna meeting will doubtless feel that their particular contributions have received scant attention and that others have been over-emphasized. We feel that this situation is an inevitable consequence of our brief and of our approach. We can only remind such colleagues that their papers have been published in full already. The book which follows is the joint attempt of two ecologists of rather different previous experience who have enjoyed the unusual (if not unique!) privilege of listening to and arguing with some sixty or seventy colleagues, brought together on this occasion by the PT sectional committee, with financial support from UNESCO, the Polish Academy of Sciences and many IBP national committees. We have tried to discharge the debt which we owe, in exchange for this experience, by a synthesis rather than a report. We believe that this is what is needed most by practising ecologists who are carrying out the hard work of implementing the International Biological Programme.

K. Petrusewicz
A. Macfadyen

November 1969

1

The Idea of Productivity

What are productivity studies? Why do we set them apart from other ecological investigations? Why are they currently fashionable and considered so important that they have been accepted by the International Biological Programme (IBP) as one of the principal fields of biological study?

There seem to us to be two important answers to such questions.

(1) In productivity studies, ecological units are analysed as bioenergetic systems, and thus fundamental productivity concepts are necessary for an understanding of the balance between a population's intake and output of matter and energy.

(2) At the basis of productivity studies lies the distinction between the concept of production (P) and that of standing crop. The perception of this difference has made it essential to introduce and define the concept of turnover (Θ), which is fundamental for our understanding of ecological processes.

These two facts have helped us to obtain a new and deeper insight into the economy of nature, the functioning of ecological units, as well as the ecological role (niche) of the species under study. We shall try to explain this in some more detail.

1.1 The basic concepts of an energy budget

The ability to produce organic matter from simple mineral compounds is, on our globe, the exclusive property of photosynthetic autotrophs—the plants.* They produce energy-rich organic matter with the aid of the radiant

---

* For the sake of simplicity we ignore chemotrophs, firstly because theirs is an insignificant role (Winberg, 1960; Macfadyen, 1963a), for example according to Winberg (1960) their production of organic material in lakes accounts for as little as 1·5 per cent of photosynthesis, and secondly because most of them draw energy from compounds of organic origin.

energy reaching the earth from the sun. The potential energy contained in the organic matter produced by plants furnishes the basis for the life of all animals, man included. Plant-consuming animals (or herbivores) absorb the potential energy fixed in organic matter and rearrange it into their own calorie-rich tissue and also utilize a part of it for their vital processes, and thus dissipate it as heat (entropy). In the final analysis, therefore, the life of all animals, man included, depends on plants. Man, who has learned how to put sputniks into circumterrestrial orbits, how to send men to the moon and rockets to the planets, photograph them and transmit the pictures back to the earth, the very man who has learned all this and has now control over immeasurable quantities of nuclear energy has in order to be able to live, to consume the solar energy fixed by plants in organic matter.

When analysing the fate of the energy-rich organic matter consumed, rearranged, and utilized either directly by herbivores or indirectly by carnivores we can distinguish the following basic concepts relating to productivity ecology.

Food potentially available to any population is either ignored or else it is killed, i.e. removed from a previous trophic level (MR). The material removed (MR) by any trophic unit—an individual, population, group of populations or trophic group, or, finally, a trophic level—is very rarely all utilized. A part of it, usually a large one, is not utilized (NU), and a part is consumed (Fig. 1.1); the latter is referred to as consumption (C), some of which is eliminated chiefly as faeces and the products of nitrogen metabolism, primarily urine, and is described as rejecta (FU). The remaining part, described as assimilation (A) is utilized by the trophic unit (organism, population) in part for building up its own tissue and reproductive products— referred to as production (P)—and in part for its vital processes. Since the latter is usually measured in terms of oxygen (O_2) uptake and/or carbon dioxide elimination, it is described as respiration (R) (Fig. 1.1).

All this may be summed up in three basic equations describing the energy balance of a biological (trophic) unit—whether an organism or a population:

$$MR = NU + C \dotfill 1.1$$
$$C = P + R + FU \dotfill 1.2$$
$$A = P + R \dotfill 1.3$$

from which it is possible to derive a number of further equations, such as:
$P = A - R = C - (R + FU)$.

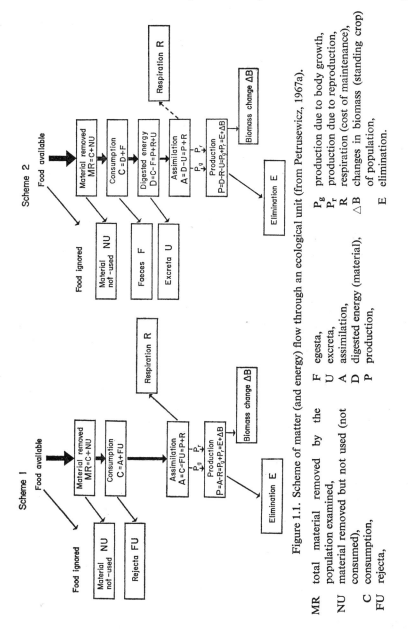

Figure 1.1. Scheme of matter (and energy) flow through an ecological unit (from Petrusewicz, 1967a).

MR total material removed by the population examined,
NU material removed but not used (not consumed),
C   consumption,
FU rejecta,

F   egesta,
U   excreta,
A   assimilation,
D   digested energy (material),
P   production,

P_g production due to body growth,
P_r production due to reproduction,
R   respiration (cost of maintenance),
$\triangle B$ changes in biomass (standing crop) of population,
E   elimination.

Let us first consider assimilation. This is the part of matter (energy) which becomes involved in the metabolism of the trophic unit (population) and is utilized by it. Hence it is often described as energy flow.

This is a simplified scheme. Many physiologists would protest on the ground that faeces, which consist of matter that has merely passed through the alimentary tract without becoming involved in metabolic processes, must not be put into the same category as urine, which is the product of metabolism and was thus for a time a constituent part of the tissues of the trophic unit considered (consuming organism). To this one may object by pointing out that the part of the material consumed which is eliminated as urine remains in the tissues only briefly and thus merely passes through the organism; it is eliminated every few hours and does not accumulate in an organism as production. However, the term 'briefly' is subjective. The fact remains that what is eliminated as urine was for some time a component part of an organism, was in the blood stream, and, consequently, part of the tissue of the trophic unit (organism) considered. The physiological criterion, in fact, fails us. What makes it legitimate for ecologists to group faeces and urine together and cover them by the single term rejecta (FU) is the following argument: the term designates that part of the energy contained in consumption (C) which has not been utilized by the trophic unit (organism, population) but has entered it (an organism) and then left as energy-containing matter. An additional practical and methodological argument is the fact that with a vast majority of animals urine and faeces are eliminated together and can therefore not be measured separately without chemical analysis.

The concept of rejecta (FU), which is equal to faeces plus urine is convenient and—as meaning consumed but non-utilized energy—makes sense with regard to the purpose of our investigations even though it is arbitrary. And it needs to be borne in mind that we cannot avoid using such arbitrary terms. Take for instance faeces: what we are dealing with and measuring in actual experiments is not, strictly speaking, 'that part of food that has not been digested', because it contains a certain quantity of digestive juices, epithelial cells of the intestines, and the like. Nevertheless it does make sense to subtract the empirically determined quantity of faeces from the food eaten because this gives us the trophic unit's net intake of matter (energy).

If required for more detailed investigations, e.g. for productivity studies of one individual, and especially in the analysis of cycles of matter (especially the circulation of mineral elements), we may consider separately: (1) egesta (F) as that part of consumption that is eliminated as faeces, rumen gas, or regurgitated, and (2) digested energy (material) (D) as the biomass incorporated into the organism (population), including material excreted with urine or through the skin, all for a given time and space. A part of the digested energy (D) will be eliminated as excreta (U), and the other part assimilated (A). Here the principal equations of the metabolic balance will take the following forms (see Fig. 1.1, scheme 2):

$$C=P+R+U+F=D+F \dotfill 1.4$$
$$D=P+R+U=A+U \dotfill 1.5$$

As may be seen, the basic concepts involved in productivity studies are elements of the energy budget (balance) of a trophic unit (trophic level, trophic group, population, organism). They are concepts reflecting the levels of income and expenditure in the metabolic balance of the unit investigated, the continuous natural processes of ingestion of food rich in energy, its conversion into the consumer's own energy-rich tissue (including production of offspring) as well as utilization for maintenance. And this is the first specific difference distinguishing productivity studies from other ecological investigations, which deal only with total ecological units.

1.2 Production (P), standing crop (B) and turnover Θ

In 'classical' ecological investigations, such as those concerned with the dynamics of populations, the structure of trophic levels, the quantitative relations between trophic levels (e.g., Elton's pyramid of numbers) and similar concepts, the basic quantity was the standing crop. In (often very interesting) studies of population dynamics, however, the basic quantity is the size of a population, i.e., the numbers (N) of organisms present at any particular moment on a given area (standing crop in terms of individuals). This quantity can be determined empirically with varying accuracy depending on the species, refinement of the method, and the time we are able to spend (see also 3.1). When sufficiently frequent, these determinations will tell us a great deal about the population in question: they will enable its dynamic changes to be followed, and such features as the time and magnitude of seasonal maximum and annual increase to be established. But even the most meticulously collected numerical data tell us little, often nothing at all, about how many animals man or any other predator could remove over a certain period of time, e.g., annually. For even the most accurate curve of numerical dynamics does not tell us how many discrete individuals (v) passed through the given population (were present in the population for only a particular period of time). Plotted as connecting points that represent the known values of actual census figures, the curve of population dynamics merely gives the difference between natality and mortality. An increase by five individuals may be the result of addition of five individuals at zero mortality, or of 10 individuals at a mortality of five, or of 50 individuals with the loss of 45.

When the numbers and weights of individuals are known we are able to calculate the biomass (standing crop—B), i.e., the weight of all the organisms composing the trophic unit in question, which are present at any given moment per unit of space (in the area under investigation). The changes in biomass (ΔB) reflect the overall effect of additions and losses of individuals together with changes in their weight (individual growth). We can also express the biomass in terms of energy, obtaining more uniform and thus more comparable values. But all this tells us nothing about the mass that has been produced or lost by the particular trophic unit during the period of study.

Let us try to make this clear with the aid of a few models. The simplest analogy to the relation between production and biomass is that of a body of water with inflow and outflow (Fig. 1.2). The volume of water in the body represents the standing crop or biomass (B), the volume of inflow represents

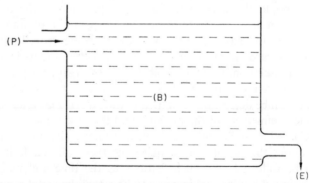

Figure 1.2. Model of standing crop and production.

Water inflow represents production, P (or number of individuals born); water level (or volume) represents the standing crop, B (or numbers N); and water outflow represents elimination, E.

production (P). When the outflow is stopped (in the absence of any losses, a situation not usually met with in nature), the difference in the volume of water in that body (which corresponds to the difference in biomass ΔB) reflects accurately the inflow of water. But when inflow and outflow balance each other exactly, the volume of water in the body will not change ($\Delta B = \Theta$). Even when measured with the greatest accuracy, the volume tells us nothing about the inflow (production).

For another example of the relation between production and biomass let us take a hypothetical curve of population biomass or changes in the number of individuals plotted from absolutely complete data (Fig. 1.3). It will show us that production is the total amount of tissue substance* produced over a definite period of time (body growth and reproduction), irrespective of whether it has survived to the end of that period or not. It can be written as

$$P = \Delta B + E \quad \dots\dots\dots\dots\dots\dots\dots\dots\dots\dots\dots\dots\dots\dots\dots\dots \quad 1.6$$

where E stands for elimination, i.e., the biomass of individuals that have died or been killed or otherwise removed as well as losses through moulting, web or cocoon production, and the like, but not through respiration.

In terms of individuals the equation may be written

$$v_+ = \Delta N + v_E = (N_T - N_0) + v_E \quad \dots\dots\dots\dots\dots\dots\dots\dots\dots\dots \quad 1.7$$

where v_+ is the number of the individuals that were added to the population considered during time-period T, v_E is the number of individuals removed (eliminated) during time T, and N_0 and N_T are the numbers of individuals composing the population at the beginning and end of time T.

On the other hand, the equation for total number of discrete individuals, i.e. the number of physical organisms which occurred at any time in a population during time period T regardless of whether they survived or not to the end of the period of observation, may be written as

$$v = N_0 + v_+ = N_T + v_E \quad \dots\dots\dots\dots\dots\dots\dots\dots\dots\dots\dots\dots\dots \quad 1.8$$

Distinction between the concept of production (P), or the discrete number of the individuals, and that of standing crop leads us to the concept of turnover. Odum (1959) distinguishes turnover rate—the fraction of the total

* For accuracy one should add: 'and not utilized for vital processes (R)'.

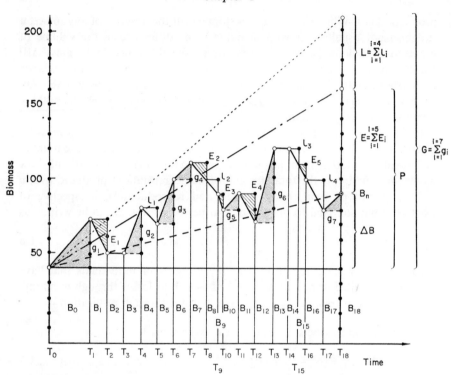

Figure 1.3. Model of changes in biomass and production (from Petrusewicz 1967a).

Let us imagine that the curve is based on an ideal set of information so that all changes of biomass have been recorded and presented graphically (i.e. records were sufficiently frequent so that, during the intervals between them, there were either increases or decreases but not both). E, elimination (due to death, loss of body material, emigration); L, weight loss; 1, consecutive weight losses.

amount of substance (number of individuals, biomass, quantity of particular elements, e.g. phosphorus, nitrogen etc.) which enters (or is released) in a specified period of time—from turnover time, which is the reciprocal of turnover rate and designates the length of time needed for the complete exchange of an existing number of individuals, amount of biomass, or particular elements of biomass. For example, if 200 units are present at one time and 10 leave or enter each day the turnover rate is $^{10}/_{200}$ or 0·05 or 5 per cent per day.

If $\bar{t}'$ is the average time that individuals existed at any time in the population during period of time T, the ratio $T : \bar{t}'$ will tell us what fraction of the average number of individuals was exchanged during time T; this will be the turnover rate or, in short, turnover during time T:

$$\Theta_{NT} = \frac{T}{\bar{t}'} \dots\dots\dots\dots\dots\dots\dots\dots\dots\dots\dots\dots\dots\dots 1.9a$$

or, if we accept T as a unit (and use it to measure $\bar{t}'$), then turnover of individuals is:

$$\Theta_N = \frac{1}{\bar{t}'} \dots\dots\dots\dots\dots\dots\dots\dots\dots\dots\dots\dots\dots\dots 1.9b$$

It can be readily seen (Petrusewicz, 1966, see also 3.1.4) that:

$$v = \bar{N}.\Theta_{NT} = \bar{N}.\frac{T}{\bar{t}'} \dots\dots\dots\dots\dots\dots\dots\dots\dots\dots\dots\dots 1.10$$

In some investigations we may be interested in defining the turnover of biomass, that is the fraction of biomass which was exchanged during the time interval T:

$$\Theta_T = \frac{P}{B} \dots\dots\dots\dots\dots\dots\dots\dots\dots\dots\dots\dots\dots 1.11a$$

or, when time T is very short

$$\Theta = \frac{P}{B} \dots\dots\dots\dots\dots\dots\dots\dots\dots\dots\dots\dots\dots 1.11\,b*$$

Turnover of biomass and turnover of individuals are related quantities but not identical. In comparing them we wish to make the following three points.

1. Turnover of biomass is the more complicated quantity. Whereas turnover of individuals (Θ_N) designates the rate of exchange of individuals (units) of a population, biomass turnover covers exchange of individuals (units) and growth of individuals. Its reciprocal, therefore, does not indicate the time of presence of individuals and is not usually investigated.

2. Turnover of individuals Θ_N multiplied by $\bar{N}$ (equation 1.10) gives us the total number of discrete individuals which were present in the population

---

* Widely known in Soviet literature as 'P to B coefficient' (Ivlev, 1945; Winberg, 1960).

during unit time (for any fraction of time T) $v = N_0 + v_+$ where v_+ is the number of individuals entering the population (born and immigrated) within the time interval T; on the other hand, turnover of biomass multiplied by $\bar{B}$ gives us the production, i.e., only the increase of biomass (see 3.1.4).

3.   If we revert to the model of the water body (Fig. 1.2), Θ expresses the ratio of water inflow to the volume of water in the body. We can also imagine, turnover of outflow (turnover of elimination): $\Theta_E = E : \bar{B}$, which is a very interesting quantity expressing the rate of elimination of the existing biomass. Logically (though we have not met with it in published research work) we can also imagine the ratio of the inflow-outflow balance to the biomass:

$$\frac{P+E}{2} : \bar{B}$$

To summarize: it is evident that numbers (N), i.e. number of animals present at any time moment, and number of discrete individuals (v) which occurred at any time during period T are totally different concepts. And this is also why we have designated the last concept by a completely different symbol v (the Greek 'n', pronounced 'nu').

Number of discrete individuals, as well as production and other productivity concepts are values which are cumulative in time, whereas in summing up standing crops we obtain a meaningless quantity. The number of discrete individuals and production as cumulative values reflect the continuous process of inflow and outflow of individuals or biomass (energy) in a population, whereas standing crops and their changes reflect merely the end results and do not give a picture of energy flow and matter cycling. And this is also why we have stated that the introduction of the turnover concept, and the distinction between the production and discrete number of individuals on the one hand, and the standing crop on the other hand—regardless of whether the latter is expressed as numbers, biomass or energy—lies at the basis of productivity studies, and permits us to obtain a new and deeper insight into the processes of the economy of nature.

1.3   Types of productivity studies and their objectives

Productivity studies may relate to an individual as well as to an ecological unit. The former studies lie rather within the compass of physiology, and the information they supply—together with such ecological characteristics of a population as size, sex ratio and age structure—serve in productivity studies of ecological units merely as empirical starting data. From these data, which are obtained through experiment and observation we may derive, by reasoning based on theoretical assumptions and models, the values pertaining to the different productivity concepts*.

The procedure usually involves the use of the demographic quantities employed in population ecology, such as average population size ($\bar{N}$), number of individual-days ($\bar{N}.T$), length of life ($\bar{t}$), rate of mortality (η), natality (b), etc., and only by suitably combining them with the relevant physiological data can we construct a method of estimating the quantities sought. The word 'estimating', and not 'calculating', is here used deliberately because, in contrast with investigations of the productivity of individuals, in which fairly accurate data can be obtained, it is usually only possible in productivity studies of populations to estimate such quantities as production and assimilation and not calculate them, even when working with laboratory populations. Many of the difficulties arise from the need to find the best possible way of applying laboratory data to field populations.

The principal purpose of productivity studies is not usually to calculate or estimate—often in itself a very difficult and complicated task—any of the quantities here involved alone. The real aim is to compare the results of a large series of analyses of efficiency and rate and ratio of productivity concepts, within as well as between trophic levels. This should lead to the discovery and comparison of the paths and (the most important of all) the magnitude of the energy flow in different populations.

Productivity studies are a rather young branch of ecology. The earliest publications, which mainly related to aquatic habitats (hydrobiology), appear in the 1930's, for example Juday and Shomer (1935), Winberg (1934, 1936) and Borutzky (1939). In the field of limnology the first attempts to draw up energy flow schemes for entire ecosystems appeared in the 1940's (e.g. Juday, 1940; Ivlev, 1942). These were followed by further generalizations involving comparisons between the efficiency, production and activity of whole trophic levels and ecosystems (Lindemann, 1942; Macfadyen, 1948, 1963–1st Ed., 1957; Odum, 1959–1st Ed., 1953; Clarke, 1954; and Winberg, 1960). Although the productivity studies were mainly developed from the field of limnology, one can also find productivity ideas in studies of terrestrial

---

* In studies of the productivity of ecological units, especially in the field, only some of the relevant quantities, e.g., consumption (C) or egesta (F), can be determined empirically (see 5.2), and even these only exceptionally.

ecosystems and especially in those of soil organisms. Bornebusch's study (1930) was perhaps the first to compare activity of species on the basis of metabolism but was followed only much later by more detailed work on major groups such as that of Nielsen (1949, 1961) on nematodes and enchytraeids. It is only recently, however, that the first attempts to synthesise the data for whole terrestrial ecosystems have been possible (e.g. Cragg, 1961; Macfadyen, 1963b). It has become a major task for the International Biological Programme to collect sufficient examples of such studies for critical comparisons to be made in the future.

Even though productivity studies are so young, they are very diverse. It is hardly an exaggeration to say that almost every research worker, or at least every research school has its own theme. However, broadly speaking, the work may be said to be developing along three principal lines of approach.

(a) The first approach concerns the energy budget of individual populations (occasionally trophic groups). The purpose here is to determine as accurately as possible the relevant component quantities of the energy budget (C, P, R, A, and FU) and to use them to compare the efficiencies of various species from either different systematic groups (for instance, homoiotherms *versus* poikilotherms, vertebrates *versus* invertebrates, and so forth) or to contrast different trophic groups, e.g., herbivores *versus* carnivores, or herbivores *versus* detritophages.

The indices of efficiency most commonly used for comparisons, using the nomenclature of Wiegert (1964) are:
assimilation/consumption efficiency (A/C),
production/assimilation efficiency (P/A),
production/consumption efficiency ('ecological efficiency', P/C).

Also ratios, e.g. P/R and Pr/Pg (or Pr/P and Pg/P) as well as turnover rate P/B̄ are more and more often used for sometimes very interesting comparisons. This information gives us deeper insight into the ecological niche of a species and its biology, and enables us to look at its evolutionary adaptation from a new angle.

(b) The second approach is the analysis of particular food chains, knowledge of which—(rather more than of the magnitude of standing crop)—leads to a better understanding of the ecological role of a particular population. When based on the standing crop (numbers N, or biomass B), Elton's pyramid has frequently proved to be inverted, which does not occur when productivity concepts are used to construct it.

In these studies, starting from the ecological unit (population) under analysis, we may proceed in two directions—'upwards', or 'downwards', in terms of trophic relations.

When proceeding 'upwards' (e.g. from plant to carnivore), the quantity we are most interested in will be production (P), or elimination (E), i.e., what the 'prey' population may 'offer' to the 'consuming' population. In practical terms this may refer to animals which are exploited in one way or another by man, but in theory it may concern any prey population. The most useful indices other than P and E may be quantities such as $C_{\lambda 2}/P_{\lambda 1}$, where $C_{\lambda 2}$=consumption of predator and $P_{\lambda 1}$=production by prey, and yield/production (Y/P).

When we go 'downwards', i.e., when we consider the analysed population as predators, we may be interested in the ecological pressure which is exerted by a population upon its prey, i.e., in number of prey consumed. However, this pressure is better estimated by measuring the material removed (MR) rather than that of consumption (C). As is well known, the body of the prey is rarely eaten completely, as is the case, for example, when a viper swallows an entire mouse or frog; most often some part, sometimes a major part, of the prey is not used (NU). An explicit example of such a situation is a beaver felling a whole tree in order to eat the bark from the small branches. A good estimate of the influence on the preceding link in the food chain can be a ratio $MR_{\lambda}/P_{\lambda-1}$, which designates the ecological pressure which it exerts on the trophic level below it, or $C_{\lambda}/P_{(\lambda-1)}$. This is the degree of the utilization of the production of the lower level, or $P_{\lambda}/P_{(\lambda-1)}$, which is the proportion of matter (energy) retained after passage from the lower level to the higher one.

In practical terms, man may be interested to know what proportion of the production of a lower level is 'stolen' by pests or rival predators, i.e., the competitors of man which feed on the product utilized either by man (e.g. grain crops, or vegetables) or by populations exploited by man (e.g. orthopterans as the competitors of sheep or cattle). From a theoretical viewpoint, greater depth is added to our knowledge of the ecological role of the population analysed.

(c) The third approach is concerned with analysis of the functional properties of ecosystems, in which the knowledge of the energy flow is of paramount importance. As Macfadyen (1967) puts it, the cardinal purpose is here 'to compare the overall energy flow throughout whole populations in order to assess the relative importance of competing species within a trophic level, of successive levels in an ecosystem and of one ecosystem with another. Energy flow can also be used as a powerful tool in assessing quantitatively the effects of more intangible interactions between species as for instance in the case of the promotion of microbial activity in decomposer systems through the stimulating effects of different components of the fauna.

In such cases, involving measurements on many species and in relation to all the complexity of a natural environment, we are rarely able to achieve a high level of accuracy and the details of energy and biomass partition within a population of each particular species are relatively unimportant. In such cases the amount of energy involved in production of body tissues is usually small in comparison with the total energy flow through the population. We shall not go seriously astray if we make use of respiration figures in place of true assimilation figures which, as we shall see, are often rather difficult to obtain.

In studies concerned with the functioning of entire ecosystems generalization may be pushed even further. With some approximation it may be assumed that the average amount of biomass (standing crop) at a particular season, e.g., in spring, does not differ very significantly between years. For major periods of time this is not an unreasonable assumption, and it is legitimate for us in such theoretical studies to add up the whole respiration of heterotrophic organisms and compare it with primary production.

Studies of this kind, although very approximate, are important as a source of theoretical ideas and generalization on which to base future research.

Although in research, especially in the case of the third approach, it is often permissible to estimate the energy flow (A) as costs of maintenance (R), or even to estimate entropy ($\approx$R) for two or more trophic levels jointly when we wish to call attention to the fundamental significance of the value of determining production. Certainly, production estimates are the basis for calculating other quantities, such as consumption and respiration, for these are the result of the vital function of an entire population, and this is composed of the starting biomass (B_0) and of production; the former is, after a long period of time, so small in relation to the latter as to enable us to ignore it and ascribe all assimilation, respiration, etc., exclusively to the production (provided that emigration and immigration either do not exist or balance each other). But this is not the main point we have in mind here. Production is the measure of retention of energy in an ecosystem and is, therefore, in the balance of ecosystems' functions, a positive quantity, unlike respiration which is a negative quantity as it is the measure of the diffusion of energy. It is thus an indication of the efficiency with which energy is utilized in an ecosystem on passage from one trophic level through another one. And surely a fundamental condition of the continued functioning of an ecosystem is precisely this efficiency, which is as necessary for the elaboration or diversification of the system's structure as is the retention of energy in it.

2

Measurements, Units in Productivity Studies, their Definitions and Symbols

2.1 About terminology in general

The difficulties that bedevil biologists in general and ecologists in particular when they seek to define concepts and settle terminology are not a matter of accident. We deal with highly complicated concepts, which have many aspects, and we try at the same time to make the definition reflect the diversity of the aspects of the concept, and thus represent a genuine generalization. In these circumstances an equating definition, especially in its classic form*, is not up to the task, even if there should be no disagreement among ecologists concerning the essence of the concepts involved. Almost any of the concepts expressing certain sets of aspects of a biological process can be given a number of completely different definitions, each of them true, and each of them unique in the sense that it does not fit directly any other concept. Consider, for instance, the term 'Production' (P), which is discussed further below (2.2.1), and for which we give five different definitions, each of them characterizing different ecological views of the concept in question. In the case of concepts of such great complexity any attempt to construct an exhaustive definition would mean trying to compress into a single grammatical sentence a sequence of predicating theses—a difficult task, and one not really likely to produce a very 'readable' result. So the result is not always worth the labour, and in such cases one is surely well advised to give up only one equating definition, especially the classic one, and define the concept by giving a number of different descriptions, or definitions, each of them dealing with a different aspect, with the express condition, however, that none of them should conflict with any other. On the contrary, they should all be mutually complementary in the sense that they should contribute to the

* According to logic an equating definition, which presumes equality of the *definiendum* with the *definiens*, is the reply to the question 'what is X?' 'X is . . .', and the classic form of the equating definition is '*per genus proximum et differentiam specificam*'.

comprehension of the concept as an integrated whole. For we should bear in mind that what we are defining is not some detached, isolated phenomenon, but the multiplicity of aspects of a concept.

The difficulties referred to are formidable, but of a formal semantic character; they are invariably attendant upon the process of definition, even when there is agreement of views on the scope and essence of the concepts defined. Among ecologists, though, agreement is usually wanting both with regard to the scope and to the properties of the concept. Yet the definition, which states the important properties and seeks to clarify them, is really a theoretical synthesis. Differences in terminology need not necessarily be an evil, for they may reflect differences in theoretical views—a thing which is inevitable in science and good in itself. Nonetheless they make it difficult to communicate, and thus also hinder the development of research. There are good reasons for the confusion in terminology, and we shall try to indicate only some of those most frequently met with.

Very often definition and terminology cannot be agreed upon owing to important differences of views on the substance of a concept, the object. An example of this is the differences of views on what constitutes a population, which is construed by some as an 'integrated entity', and by others as a 'loose assemblage of individuals occurring together'. Although they prevent a synthesis acceptable to all, such disagreements do not make it impossible to say what, physically, is referred to and do not, therefore, make it impossible to communicate, for the object is the same in scope and differs only in associated properties.

Terminological confusion arises exceedingly often, especially in ecology, when different yet partly overlapping concepts involved in intricate and interlocking processes are distinguished and are then not kept apart or are called by the same name. A case in point is when assimilation is referred to by some as consumption less egesta $(C - F)$, and by others as consumption less rejecta $[C - (F + U)]$ (see 1.1), or when production is described in one place as the total amount of tissue produced and in another as assimilation less respiration (see definition of production and total biomass growth, 2.2.1). The tangle of concepts and terms employed in relation to production and similar notions has been demonstrated and tabulated by Macfadyen (1963a).

Research requirements may not infrequently make it essential to distinguish concepts having different but partly overlapping meanings. Where this is the case the particular concept considered, together with its scope, should be so defined as to enable it to be identified even by those who do not agree with some properties that are predicated of it.

Another source of confusion may be simply some distinction wrongly made, or some peculiarities mistakenly predicated. This cannot be helped; one either has to convince the other party or to 'shrug it off' and to rely on the social character of cognition and the practical roads along which reception of scientific information takes place, as well as on history.

Synonymy is truly a nightmare for ecologists. In fact, ecologists are conspicuously obsessed by terminology and by the belief that 'my term, or my definition is better'. So much so, indeed, that there seems to be quite a grain of truth in the jocular definition that 'ecology is that which I do and you don't', coined by Varley at the Secondary Productivity Meeting (Warsaw, 1966). But this is indeed hardly a virtue, and efforts should be made to avoid it.

Difficulties over definitions also arise when we are dealing with stochastic processes, that is processes which are more or less likely but not necessarily always inevitable.

To this we have to add the not uncommon situations in which the scope of the concept under study is of necessity determined not by logic but by the technical research opportunities, and the fact that more often than not only estimates and not exact calculations are possible.

But in spite of all these difficulties, if ecologists wish to be understood and to communicate, at least some of the more commonly used concepts will eventually have to be given a unique definition which will have to be made generally acceptable. Attention should be focused first and foremost on the scope of a concept, so that it may be identified. In selecting characteristic features efforts should not be spared to find at least those which identify what is meant in broad outlines and in physical fact. At the same time they should be acceptable to the largest possible group of those interested in the subject. This will often imply the need to omit from the definition quite important qualities, and thus to abandon a satisfactory theoretical synthesis; but it is better to leave this synthesis to the reader's own ingenuity than help perpetuate the present confusion and arguments. At this point we may as well add that we regard symbols and their uniform use as no less important than definitions. This view seems to be strikingly vindicated in section 4.2.1, where the use of the same symbols and some mathematical transformations demonstrated a striking similarity of the equations used to calculate the number of new individuals produced (v_r) for such diverse groups as rotifers (Edmondson, 1960; Hillbricht-Ilkowska, 1967), small rodents (Golley, 1960; Petrusewicz, 1968), and planktonic crustaceans (Winberg, Pečen and Šuškina, 1965), A verbal definition can always be agreed upon, provided the meaning is consistent.

One further point: when concepts relating to a process were defined, we strove to distinguish such as would be amenable to analysis if full information were available, i.e., model concepts. If actual research practice (technique, knowledge of methods) makes it necessary to use alternative data which approximate to the desired quantity, it is important to indicate the relation between the measurements made and the concepts being investigated.

In questions of terminology we have based our terms primarily on those already used, giving preference to those of Latin origin as being the more universally understood (e.g., 'consumption', and not 'food intake'), and in our choice of symbols we were guided by the desire to select those most readily associated with the term which they are to denote.

2.2   List of definitions and symbols of more important concepts

2.2.1   Concepts of ecological productivity *sensu stricto*

Note 1. All the productivity concepts, being cumulative values within time, always refer to a defined period of time (time unit, study period) and to a definite space (e.g. 1 ha, 1 m^2, defined population).

Note 2. These concepts, when they refer to energy balance should be expressed in units convertible into calories.

Note 3. Concepts concerning ecological productivity *sensu stricto* can be applied to an individual, a population, and to other ecological units which belong to the same trophic level.

PRODUCTIVITY   A general concept to cover all aspects of the rate of generation of matter or energy by production processes.

2.2.1.1   *Main concepts of metabolic balance*

P—PRODUCTION   The net balance of food transferred to the tissue of a population during a defined time period, i.e. net balance between assimilation and respiration.

$$P = A - R$$

or: the biomass (energy) accumulated (ΔB) by a population through growth and reproduction during the time in question plus matter (energy) lost in other ways than by respiration (i.e. plus elimination):

$$P = \Delta B + E$$

or: the total amount of body tissue generated by a population less weight losses:

$$P = G - L$$

or: production due to reproduction (of new born) and production of body growth:

$$P = P_r + P_g$$

or: total organic matter (energy) generated within the time period in question, and not lost by respiration, whether or not this matter (energy) remains in the population to the end of time of observation.

Note: this parameter is not equal to the total increase of body tissue of a population (cf. total biomass growth).

Syn.: net production, visible, realized, observable production.

P/T—PRODUCTION RATE   Production per unit of time.

dP/dT—INSTANTANEOUS PRODUCTION RATE

C—CONSUMPTION   Total intake of food by heterotrophic organisms during a defined time period:

$$C = P + R + FU$$

Syn.: ingestion, material (energy) ingested, food intake, energy intake, energy income.

A—ASSIMILATION   The sum of production and respiration, i.e. that part of food (energy) intake which is utilized by the consuming population:

$$A = R + P = C - FU$$

In other words: 'total energy flow at heterotrophic levels which is analogous to gross production of autotrophs' (Odum, 1959, p. 68).

Syn.: energy flow, gross production, metabolizable energy.

FU—REJECTA   That part of the total food intake which is not used for production and respiration:

$$FU = C - A = C - (P + R)$$

R—RESPIRATION   That part of food intake which is converted to heat and dissipated in life processes (metabolism) in defined period of time:

$$R = A - P = C - P - FU$$

Syn.: metabolism, cost of maintenance.

Note: if needed for more detailed investigation and especially in investigations of matter cycling and in productivity of an individual animal or single species population, the components of rejecta can be considered separately. Then:

F—EGESTA   That part of consumption which is rejected as faeces or regurgitated,

U—EXCRETA   Material derived from assimilation and excreted in urine or through the skin,

D—DIGESTED ENERGY   The energy equivalent of biomass incorporated into a population, including material excreted later in urine or through the skin (excluding material in faeces, or regurgitated), i.e. assimilation plus excreta.

Then, main equations of metabolic balance (cf. Fig. 1.1) take the forms:

$$C = P + R + F + U = D + F$$
$$D = P + R + U = A + U$$
$$F = C - D$$
$$FU = F + U$$

2.2.1.2   *Other productivity concepts*

E—ELIMINATION   Any loss of population biomass excluding loss of weight, i.e. predation (including that by man) death, exuviae, emigration or moulting. This is the amount of energy that is 'offered' to subsequent levels of the ecosystem.

$$E = P - \Delta B$$

L—WEIGHT LOSS Biomass used for metabolic needs within a time period when $R > A$; it equals the difference between the total biomass produced (G) and the production (P) (cf. Fig. 1.3):

$$L = G - P$$

G—TOTAL BIOMASS GROWTH The total amount of body tissue generated by a population within the time T including all losses (cf. Fig. 1.3), i.e. both elimination and weight losses:

$$G = \Delta B + E + L$$

Thus:

$$G = P + L \text{ and } A > G \geqslant P$$

In other words, G is the sum of all cumulative population weight increases (cf. Fig. 1.3)

$$G = \sum_{i=1}^{i=k} g_i$$

MR—MATERIAL REMOVED Total amount of matter removed (killed) by the investigated population from the preceding trophic level.

NU—MATERIAL REMOVED, NOT USED That part of material removed which is not consumed.

Y—YIELD The proportion of the production which is removed by a particular species (or group of species) belonging to a subsequent trophic level.

2.2.2 Concepts of general ecology used in productivity studies

2.2.2.1 *Time in ecological research*

T—absolute time period (time duration of an investigation); consecutive time periods $T_I, T_{II}, T_{III} \ldots T_n$

$T_1, T_2, T_3 \ldots T_i$ time moments
t_i—longevity, duration of life of an individual in a population
$\bar{t}$—average longevity; *ex definitione:*

$$\bar{t} = 1/v \sum_{i=1}^{i=v} t_i$$

$\bar{t}'$—average duration of presence of individuals in a population during period of observation T:

$$\bar{t}' = 1/v \sum_{i=1}^{i=v} \bar{t}'_i = \bar{N} \cdot T/v$$

t_s—duration of stage of development in organism's life-cycle, e.g.: t_p—period of pregnancy, t_e—time from eggs laying to hatching, t_{s1}—time of development of larvae of first instar etc.

2.2.2.2 *Number of animals*

N—NUMBERS (abundance)   The number of organisms in a population at the time of observation (standing crop expressed as number of individuals).
N_T—numbers at a particular moment
N_0—at the first moment under consideration
$\bar{N}$—AVERAGE NUMBERS (abundance)   Average abundance throughout the study period T; *ex definitione:*

$$\bar{N} = 1/K \sum_{i=1}^{i=K} N$$

where $\bar{N}_i$—successive observations of population numbers, K—number of records during time period T.

ν—NUMBER OF DISCRETE INDIVIDUALS The total number of discrete (recognisable, physical) individuals which during the time period T occurred at any time in the population:

$$\nu = \frac{\bar{N} \cdot T}{\bar{t}'} = N_0 + \nu_+ = N_T + \nu_E$$

ν_r—Number of animals born during period time in question
ν_E—Number of discrete animals eliminated during period time T
ν_{mg}—Number of animals entering and leaving the population by migration
ν_+—Number of individuals which entered to population during time T
   $\nu_+ = \nu_r + \nu_{mg} = N_T - N_0 + \nu_E$
ν_s—Number of individuals of development stages present during time T, e.g. ν_p—number of females pregnant, ν_e—number of eggs etc.
N_s—Number in a stage, i.e. number of animals in a stage present at a time moment, e.g. N_p—numbers of females pregnant, $N_{\female}$—numbers of females, N_e—numbers of eggs etc.
$\bar{N}T$—Quantity of individual-days

$$\bar{N}T = \nu \cdot \bar{t}' = \sum_{i=1}^{i=\nu} t'_i$$

2.2.2.3 *Weight and biomass*

W—WEIGHT Weight of an animal at a concrete time moment; usually used as the average for a set of animals investigated, or for a population or even for a species.

ΔW—change in weight during a definite time period of life Δt; $\Delta W = W_t - W_0$

$v = \Delta W / \Delta t$—absolute gain in weight
   Gain in weight of one individual per unit of time, usually per day (g/individ./day).

v'—relative gain in weight
   Gain in weight per unit time, per unit of body weight (g/g wt/day).

$q = dW/dt \cdot W$—instantaneous growth rate; if growth is exponential:

$$q = \frac{\ln W_T - \ln W_0}{\bar{t}}$$

B—BIOMASS OR STANDING CROP   In terms of mass of living organisms present in a population (or other ecological unit) at a given moment; it may be expressed as energy content (in calories) or in weight units (live, dead, dry, ash-free weight).

B̄—AVERAGE BIOMASS   Average standing crop for study period T, *ex definitione*:

$$\bar{B} = 1/K \sum_{i=1}^{i=K} B_i$$

where B_i—successive standing crop records, K—number of records.

ΔB—BIOMASS CHANGE   The difference in standing crop between any two records:

$$\Delta B = B_T - B_0$$

i.e. an increase or decrease in population biomass during the study period T (positive or negative ΔB).

B̄.T—QUANTITY OF BIOMASS-DAYS   Product of mean biomass and period of investigation.

2.2.2.4 *Natality and mortality*

L—LITTER SIZE   Number of eggs in a batch or cocoon

f—FECUNDITY RATIO   Share or percentage of pregnant females:

$$f = N_p/N_{\female}$$

s—SEX RATIO: $s = N_{\female}/N$

b—BIRTH RATE OF A POPULATION, i.e. two times number of animals born per unit time per average individual in population

$$b = v_r/\bar{N} \cdot T = \frac{s \cdot f \cdot L}{t_p}$$

β—INSTANTANEOUS BIRTH RATE; assuming β constant $N_T = N_0 \cdot e^{\beta T}$ and

$$\beta = \frac{f \cdot \ln (L \cdot s + 1)}{t_p}$$

if sex ratio 1 : 1

$$\beta = \frac{f \cdot \ln (L/2 + 1)}{t_p}$$

m—MORTALITY RATE Number of animals dying per individual, per unit of time; for species with overlapping generations:

$$m = \frac{N_0 + v_+ - N_T}{\bar{N} T} = \frac{v_E}{\bar{N} \cdot T}; \text{ for a cohort } m = \frac{N_1 - N_2}{\bar{N} \cdot T}$$

η—INSTANTANEOUS MORTALITY RATE Assuming η constant, i.e. exponential survivorship curve:

$$N_T = N_0 \cdot e^{-\eta t} \text{ and } \eta = \frac{\ln N_0 - \ln N_t}{t}$$

r—INSTANTANEOUS RATE OF POPULATION GROWTH $= \beta - \eta$.

2.2.2.5 *Turnover—Θ*

$Θ_N$—INDIVIDUAL TURNOVER The fraction of the total population which is exchanged in a given time period (T):

$$Θ_T = \frac{T}{\bar{t}}$$

or per a unit of time: $Θ = \dfrac{1}{\bar{t}}$

The most usual measure is turnover per year.

$Θ_p$—PRODUCTION TURNOVER The fraction of the total population which enters it in a given time period. This is an index of efficiency of biomass production:

$$Θ_p = \frac{P}{B}$$

Θ_E—ELIMINATION TURNOVER   The fraction of the population which is released in a given time period:

$$\Theta_E = \frac{E}{B} \text{ or } \Theta_E = \frac{E}{B}$$

2.2.3   Ecological units investigated

1. POPULATION
Totality of organisms of one single species continuously present in some particular place, at least throughout some limited period of time.

Syn.: stock (especially in fishery studies).

Note: if a group of species is investigated, it is better to use the term 'trophic group' and to describe more precisely those organisms which are being studied.

2. TROPHIC LEVEL
A set of organisms (populations) which are at a similar 'trophic distance' from producers, and have a more or less similar food source. A very ill-defined concept, which is nevertheless often indispensable both in practical research and in reasoning; when used it should be more closely defined.

3. ECOSYSTEM
A system (or totality) of organisms and their environment, occupying a space, in some way defined, and which interact to bring about an exchange of materials.

2.3   Units of measurement in productivity studies

For expressing the quantitative aspects of the basic concepts in productivity studies, such as C, P, R, A, and FU, as well as other concepts involved in these studies (e.g., biomass and elimination) we can use any arbitrary unit that is suitable for making comparisons. The measure most commonly used is weight units of biomass, i.e., kilograms of live weight (in practice this is most commonly the weight of freshly killed animals). For the sake of accuracy, chiefly in order to eliminate the differences in water content between species as well as between individuals investigated at various intervals after the moment of death, use is made of dry weight or ashfree weight, which gives the weight of organic matter. But the best and most universal measure seems to be the energy equivalent of organic matter, i.e., calories. We prefer it because it characterizes organic matter most unequivocally and is strictly comparable between different species.

Occasionally the value of biomass is given in terms of an equivalent amount of a single pure organic compound, for instance glucose. Or of the quantity of oxygen used for combustion. We do not see that this measure offers any significant advantage. It is also an estimated equivalent arrived at by calculating first the equivalent in terms of energy, which is then reconverted into units of organic substance, or oxygen.

All concepts relating to productivity should be referred to a specified space. It is evident that the production of a given species from one hectare cannot be compared with that from two hectares. But it is permissible—and often done—to refer it to the 'population analyzed', provided this population is really and effectively isolated. A case in point may be laboratory studies, in which artificial and fully isolated populations may be established. In field work the necessary conditions may be obtained when for instance the investigations cover the whole population of an island. In such cases the 'entire population' is an admissible measure; but even here space must be indicated for comparisons with other studies to be possible.

In some rather rare cases space is more appropriately indicated by volume than by area, for instance, the volume of flour occupied by the flour beetle (*Tribolium*).

Furthermore, in relation to processes, which inevitably have a time aspect, C, P, R, A, and FU, as well as other values and concepts relating to productivity, must also always be referred to a specified time. As it is impossible to compare the production from one hectare with that from two hectares, so also it is impossible to compare the matter (energy) produced (P) or consumed (C) in one year with data for half a year or fifteen months.

Two views are expressed in ecology, concerned not so much with the item itself but with the concept of 'production'. Some investigators think that two concepts should be discerned: production as quantity of matter (P) and production rate (P/T), others think that production without a defined time is a useless concept in ecological studies, and that production should always be related to time, or quantity per unit time which is rate.

The former say that both the term and the concept are necessary to define the amount of living matter produced by a population. The latter maintain that although the idea of the amount of matter produced does exist, if it is not related to time it is useless for further scientific elaboration, comparisons etc. The amount of biomass produced, if not related to a time factor is an empty concept, useless cognitively. If, however, we define production as quantity in a defined time, such a concept will not differ substantially from the production rate since, for instance, 9 kcal/1·5 year = 6 kcal/1 year.

One can say: yes, but in physics there are discrete concepts of distance and velocity. Distance is a measurable quantity, thus it is necessary to define it. On the other hand when discussing the process of motion, a time interval must be considered; in this context a distance to be travelled is inevitably related to velocity, that is distance per unit time, etc.

Personally we do not feel any need for distinguishing (in ecological investigations) quantity and rate of production. However, following numerous discussions [e.g. the Second General Assembly of IBP (Paris, 1966), Working Meeting on Principles and Methods of Secondary Productivity Studies of Terrestrial Ecosystems IBP PT (Warsaw-Jablonna, 1966), many proposals within IBP, etc.] we propose to accept:

—production (P) which is the amount of matter produced in any given time; if value P is to be used in equations balancing the energy flow, the time must be defined;

—production rate (P/T)—amount of production per unit time;

—instantaneous production rate $\dfrac{dP}{dT}$.

Many misunderstandings have also been caused by the term productivity. It is often used as: (1) synonymous with production, (2) synonymous with production rate, (3) a concept meaning potentiality for production, and (4) a general term to cover all aspects of production. In the present book the latter meaning is used.

It needs to be borne in mind that owing to the cycle of seasons in most habitats on our planet the smallest unit of time in ecological research, which cannot be subdivided into comparable units is the year; it is usually the best unit, and the one most suited for making comparisons with other studies. Obviously, for special purposes and with suitable reservations concerning comparisons any other unit of time may be used. But it must be remembered that the diurnal alternation of light and darkness creates a certain rhythm in nature which makes twenty-four hours the smallest permissible time unit, at least for the macrofauna.

Thus the concepts employed in productivity studies can be expressed in any arbitrary but comparable units considered to be proportional to a quantity of organic matter. This is best done in terms of the calorific equivalent of biomass per unit space and per unit time.

Conversion factors between different units of energy are tabulated in the Appendix (p. 159).

2.4 The hierarchy of ecological groupings investigated

Biological productivity studies may concern individuals as well as ecological units. The definition of an individual usually poses no problem, but the definition of ecological units is often more difficult. Although we meet with the term 'population' in almost every ecological work, it is very hard to find a generally acceptable definition of it, for there is no agreement on what, essentially, a population is. Possible definitions range from a 'a loose assemblage of organisms occurring together in some particular space', through those which emphasise ties between the individuals in a population, to those in which the population is defined as an integrated entity, or even endowed with the qualities of some superorganism. This probably makes it impossible to give a definition that would satisfy everybody. The futility of such attempts seems to have been abundantly demonstrated in many debates at a series of IBP sessions. Nevertheless, we cannot conveniently avoid this concept in ecological investigations and this makes it necessary to try to give a 'minimum' definition which would be acceptable for most and would not exclude a variety of other descriptions.

Such a minimum definition could be: 'an assemblage of individuals of a single species continuously present in some particular place, at least throughout some limited period of time'. Authors of this handbook would add: '. . . among which there develop ecological ties and interrelations which integrate them into a functional unit with characteristic ecological properties' whereas other researchers would not do this. However, it seems that this 'minimum' definition will serve the present purpose.

The next ecological unit within the sphere of productivity studies is the trophic level, that is a set of organisms (populations) located at a similar 'trophic distance' from producers and having more or less similar food sources. As may be seen, this is a very vague concept, and the words 'similar' (used twice) and 'more or less' are hardly compatible with the principles of good definition. Nevertheless, the concept of 'trophic level' is indispensable in research practice as well as theoretical considerations and has come into its own in ecology, being used in almost all attempts at synthesis and text-books. The energy balance of an ecosystem—one of the principal problems in biology—cannot possibly be studied without the use of this concept.

It must be remembered that the trophic level—and also the food web and food chain—are concepts relating to the trophic organization and not phylogeny of organisms. Thus, the sundew (*Drosera*) should be included with carnivorous animals among consumers of the second level.

In the classification of organisms into trophic levels, considerable practical difficulty is caused by omnivorous animals. An example is the essentially herbivorous *Apodemus flavicolis*, whose food nevertheless occasionally contains 30 per cent of insects. When the percentage is known, the animal's production as well as consumption may be suitably divided between herbivores and carnivores, but in such cases the only general principle is to use common sense and caution.

Field work very often, perhaps even usually, concerns not a single population but a group of populations which are often systematically related. It is then convenient to use the term trophic group, provided of course that the species (populations) are all members of a single trophic level.

The last ecological unit to be considered in productivity studies is the ecosystem—a system (or totality) of organisms inhabiting a somehow identifiable space and considered together with their habitat. Thus an ecosystem is composed of living organisms and their abiotic medium. When complete, it comprises (1) abiotic substances (including air), (2) producers, which convert inorganic matter into energy-rich organic matter (primary productivity), (3) consumers, chiefly animals feeding on plants and other organisms. Where necessary we distinguish among the last named: (3.1) consumers of the first order (λ_2), i.e., animals feeding on living plants (phytophages) or dead plants (detritophages), and (3.2) consumers of the second and further orders (λ_3, λ_4), i.e. carnivores (predators) and parasites, and finally, (4) the reducers, chiefly bacteria and fungi, often referred to as microconsumers or saprophages—these are heterotrophic organisms which reduce organic matter to mineral compounds assimilable by plants.

Let us note that when we investigate ecological units belonging to a single trophic level—whether population or trophic group—or the trophic level itself, we may legitimately add the energy budget components (such as consumption, production, assimilation, respiration, or rejecta) of all the constituent organisms. The sum total of the production, or consumption, of individuals will give us the production, or consumption, of a population. By the same process we may proceed from populations, or trophic groups, to the trophic level. But it is not legitimate to apply the same procedure to components of different trophic levels. If we add up, for instance, the production of the prey and that of its predator, we add to the whole production of the prey also that part of its production which remains after subtraction from the consumption of the predator of FU+R, obtaining thus a meaningless quantity.

The only quantity relating to productivity which may meaningfully be added for different trophic levels is respiration (R). The sum of the respiration of all levels, or of different levels of consumers, is the measure of entropy and can be balanced against primary production.

3

Measurement of Empirical Ecological Data and Demographic Parameters

3.1 Number of organisms

3.1.1 Numbers (N)

Numbers (or abundance, or density or standing crop expressed in terms of individual organisms) is an essential parameter in all productivity calculations. It means the number of individuals actually present at any particular moment of time $(T_1, T_3 \ldots T_i)$ per unit of area (1 m², 1 ha, etc.). Occasionally it is more convenient to consider abundance with reference to volume, for instance, in hydrobiological research, or in research on soil populations, or with reference to 'population', if that population is effectively isolated (in laboratory or on an island). But even here it is essential to indicate the water or soil surface area, or the area on which the population under consideration exists.

Abundance (N) is also of paramount importance in most other ecological research. Any graph of the dynamics of a population is essentially an interpolation among empirically established numbers. In productivity studies it is indispensable in calculations both of production and of energy flow parameters (C, A, R, and FU). At the same time, in most productivity studies, it is most important to take account at least of the following details: weight of organisms, sex ratio, and pregnancy ratio (numbers of pregnant or laying females, cocoons, etc., in relation to the total numbers of females) as well as the age ratio: proportion of individual organisms at particular stages of development or in different age classes—if such can be distinguished—or, at least, in different size classes.

Numbers must always be determined or estimated empirically for a defined site and time.

3.1.2 Determination of numbers (N)

The methods of determining population size are many and greatly varied, depending on the qualities of the species investigated, the habitat, and the technical means and time available. It is not the purpose of this handbook, devoted to productivity studies, to describe in detail the methods of estimating numbers; this is done in almost every widely based ecological work, for instance, the works by Balogh (1958a) (almost entirely devoted to methods), Allee *et al.* (1955), Macfadyen (1963a), Naumov (1963) and Southwood (1967). We shall merely give a brief outline of the principles, concentrating only on methods yielding absolute numbers, i.e., the population size per unit of space. Numerical indices, e.g. number of animals per 100 trap-days, or captures during 30 minutes etc., even when comparable and not infrequently useful in general ecology, do not make quantification of productivity possible.

Broadly speaking, and necessarily as a matter of simplification, we may divide the methods of studying numbers into the following main categories: total count, sample counts, catch-mark-recapture (CMR) methods, and various special methods.

3.1.2.1 *Total count*

Total (absolute) counts obviously represent the best method for determining numbers. Unfortunately they are practicable only in rare cases, e.g., aerial photographs of large and conspicuous animals, or counts made from an aircraft (from a helicopter even animals of the size of a hare or partridge may be counted), or from a vehicle such as a landrover, which can be used successfully for counting e.g. a total population of the red grouse (Jenkins *et al.*, 1963).

Total counts extending over a given period of time can be applied to fairly large animals where individual males can be distinguished and recognized (e.g., red dear), or to birds which defend territories when nesting.

By intensive trapping, all the individuals of the population can be captured and marked during the census period. When trapping is repeated after a certain length of time (the calendar of catches method of Petrusewicz and Andrzejewski, 1962—see Fig. 3.1) it is possible to tell which individuals occur and for how long, in the population; this would give a total count extended over a certain time, and all the newly registered, i.e. unmarked individuals would be the result of reproduction or immigration. The method was used, among others, by Adams (1959) for snowshoe hares on an island, by Evans (1949) and Petrusewicz and Andrzejewski (1962) for wild mice in an isolated building, and by Gliwicz *et al.* (1968) for an island population of *Clethrionomys glareolus* which made it possible not only to distinguish

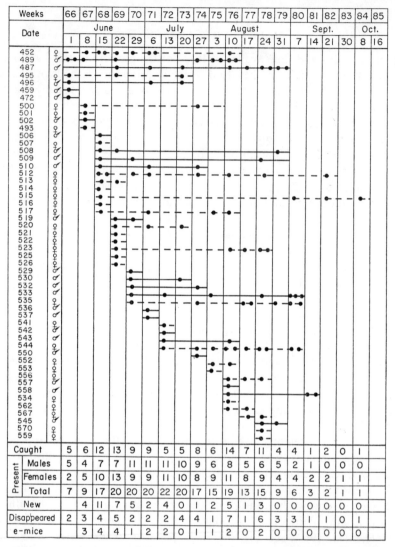

Figure 3.1. Calendar of catches (modified from Petrusewicz, Andrzejewski, 1962). Dots represent catches, the line connecting the dots — duration of presence in the study areas.

Horizontal data: life history of an individual e.g. on each occasion the place of catch can also be entered (e.g. A1, A2, B7, etc.), thus indicating the area of stay. Weight and increase in weight are obtained for a given time period. Length of stay (t'), average distance between catches (=reciprocal of real trappability), etc. can also be calculated.

Vertical data: the situation at a given moment e.g. how many individuals were caught, how many are known to be present (number of lines depicts the number of individuals present on a given day), how many were newly-caught, how many males or females, how many migrants, how many disappeared, etc.

cohorts of this continuously reproducing animal but also to follow the fate of the cohorts, and determine the ecological longevity, natality, mortality and production.

However, as has already been said, total counts are not often practicable.

3.1.2.2 *Sample counts*

This is the method most widely used in determinations of numbers; it is based on counts of all individuals of the species or group of species considered in a sample from a small but representative area, from which the quantity we are interested in is then calculated. Usually samples from several areas are collected, the population number (N) is calculated from each and then averaged by dividing the total number of samples into the sum of all N. This is Ñ—the average numbers (average standing crop in terms of individuals) for the particular moment, which is regarded in subsequent calculations as the representative numbers for the particular habitat at a particular moment in time. The basic problems that need to be resolved for each study concern: (1) appropriate selection of the sample area depending on the peculiarities of the species and habitat, (2) the number of sample units needed for the calculated average to be representative of the habitat investigated, and (3) the technique of counting individuals in a sample.

The size of the sample unit depends on the size, mobility, and abundance of the species. A sample area which is unduly small compared with the size of the organism considered may completely fail to give us an indication of its numbers. For instance, samples of 1 m², however many are taken, will not give us the numbers (N) of hare or roe deer. However, the larger the area the more time consuming becomes the procedure, the fewer are the samples that can be collected with the same amount of labour, and the less representative is the average. Hence it is advisable to choose the smallest permissible sampling areas. The expression 'smallest permissible' is very inaccurate and subjective and varies widely with the size and mobility of animals.

Very small sample areas, of the order of 0·01–0·04 m², are suitable for the animals of size of Collembola or mites (Johnson, Southwood, and Entwistle, 1952; Heikinhenno and Raatikainen, 1962) when: (1) the habitat is relatively homogeneous, and (2) the organisms investigated are fairly numerous (upwards of 50/m² and (3) do not evade capture. For animals such as the diplopods or the larvae of Elateridae surface areas of 0·25–1·0 m² may be recommended (Remane, 1958), for the large savanna insects 1–25 m² (Gillon and Gillon, 1967), and for the megafauna (e.g., small mammals) 2–6 hectares.

For hares, partridge, deer, areas of 100 ha have been recommended.

The number of sampling units to be taken depends chiefly on how homogeneous or differentiated the habitat is as well as on the numbers and character of the distribution of animals in it. In a habitat of normal heterogeneity, an average of 5–10 sampling units is usually adequately representative. In an unknown habitat one is well advised at first to collect samples from a larger number of plots and to check how many are necessary to obtain consistent population estimates.

Once the size of the sampling plots and number of units have been settled the next important point is to decide upon the technique of collecting the sample and counting the organisms in it. As regards the techniques of collecting, the trend is now towards those ensuring that all the organisms present in the sample plot are captured.

The use of so called biocenometers, usually cages of netting covering a known area, is probably the method most commonly employed for sampling meso- and macrofauna. The species investigated are collected from under such a biocenometer with an aspirator or by hand.

The really important point is that all the organisms we are concerned with should be counted as accurately as possible. The most simple way would appear to pick them up one by one. But this method is falling more and more into disuse because (1) it is very time consuming, and (2) it involves a subjective element, i.e. the researcher's personal alertness and ability. Newer developments are therefore towards mechanical devices for collecting individual organisms. The device most frequently used for the above ground invertebrate fauna is the mechanically-operated aspirator which collects the organisms into some sort of a receptacle for subsequent more leisurely counting in the laboratory.

When the results of sampling are used to estimate the numbers (N) of the animals, use is frequently made of the regression line obtained from repeated sample counts—usually three to ten—made at stated intervals from the same sample plot. The numbers of animals found in successive samples are plotted on the y-axis, against the sum of counts in the previous samples (Fig. 3.2). Usually the number of animals diminishes in a fixed proportion between individual samples and, therefore, the regression is commonly straight and the regression line and its formula can be calculated (Fig. 3.2). The point at which it bisects the x-axis gives the total number of individuals in the sample plot. This method is becoming more and more popular, but does not always yield satisfactory results. Instead of declining, the counts occasionally grow

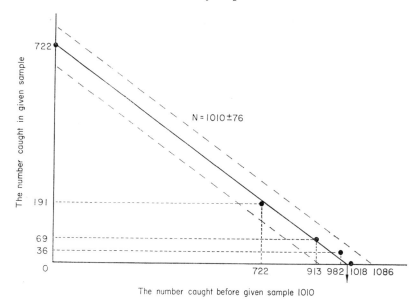

The number caught before given sample 1010

Figure 3.2. Calculation of population numbers using the regression method.
Number of hares captured in nets surrounding a 1 sq km area in successive
catches (after Andrzejewski and Jezierski, 1966).

On Ordinate: successive results of catches are plotted against the cumulative
sums of animals caught. Result of the first catch ($Y_0 = 722$) is placed on the
ordinate axis ($X = 0$ since nothing has been caught before); the second result is
plotted with $Y_1 = 191$ against $X = Y_0 = 722$ (since Y_0 has been previously caught);
the third, $Y_2 = 69$ against $X = Y_0 + Y_1 = 722 + 191 = 913$, etc. Intersection of the
abscissa axis by the regression line gives the total number of animals present N
(together with those which were not caught). In addition, the range of error can be
calculated.

between consecutive samples. According to Calhoun (1964) this may be the
result of dominance relations. When the dominant species has been eliminated
with the first samples there may be an increase in the number of captures
of the subdominant, which was not caught in the presence of the former. If
this is the case, sampling must be so intensified as to offset the effects of
inter- and intra-specific relations (increase the chances of every individual
being captured), or, alternately, the successive census figures must be simply
added up, without trying to plot the regression line.

Nevertheless, the regression analysis method is more and more commonly
used. It is also practicable with larger sample plots—one to six hectares—for

determining the numbers (N) of such animals as small mammals, reptiles, or amphibians. Samples may be collected with the aid of traps or by hand.

By setting snap traps grid fashion at 15 metre intervals in an area of six hectares, Grodziński, Pucek and Ryszkowski (1966) captured within three to five days 92 per cent of the individuals present in the investigated area (this is accepted by the 'IBP Small Mammals Centre' as the 'standard minimum' method for small rodents of temperate forests).

It should be noted that the method of collecting samples from an 'open' area—although the only one practicable for determination of the numbers of some forms—harbours many dangers, because: (1) there is doubt whether all individuals have been captured (here the regression curve is often helpful), (2) it is hard to decide how large the area from which the trapped animals come really is, and (3) there may be immigration during the census-taking period. A partial remedy for the third difficulty is to keep the census period as short as possible by intensive trapping, which will reduce errors due to possible immigration. Andrzejewski and Jezierski (1966) screened off an area of 1 km² with a net and had several people walk across it three to four times to flush the hares. The number of hares that were caught in the netting on each drive gave a clear regression curve and made it possible to determine the number of the animals in one square kilometre as well as the standard deviation (Fig. 3.2).

There is now a considerable volume of literature relating to the accuracy of determination of numbers with the aid of aspirators and the simple regression curve (e.g., Johnson, Southwood and Entwistle, 1957; Balogh, 1958a).

Another widely used method, especially for insects hatching in soil, is that of attracting organisms with so-called 'photoeclectors', usually dark cones with a single illuminated opening.

The methods used for the study of soil organisms (see Balogh, 1958; Murphy, 1962; Phillipson in press) depend very much on the habits of the species, but in almost all cases it is necessary to remove samples of known areas and extract the fauna in the laboratory.

In the case of large soft-bodied species such as *Lumbricidae* such a procedure is most destructive of the habitat and other methods are inefficient. Satchell (1955, 1962) and Raw (1960) have, however, combined the use of hand sorting with that of applying an electric current or irritant chemicals to the soil which cause many worms to come to the surface. Parallel studies employing careful hand-sorting, application of irritants and measurement of climatic factors, revealed systematic relationships between the last two. Thus it is possible, by regression analysis, to derive correction factors for different climatic conditions.

Air-living animals, such as arthropods, can be removed from soil by subjecting a sample to a gradient in a 'dry funnel' (Tullgren, 1918) heated from above. In this case, most animals move from hot, dry conditions to the damp-cool bottom of the funnel, where they are captured. It is necessary to vary the conditions according to type of soil and behaviour of the animals and many types of extractor are now used (Haarløv, 1947; Macfadyen, 1953, 1961, 1962; Kempson *et al.*, 1964).

Small animals which live in water films in the soil (*Protozoa, Nematoda*) are usually extracted in 'wet funnels' (Baermann, 1912; Nielsen, 1948; O'Connor, 1955) in which the sample is soaked in water and heated from above. The animals sink in the water and are removed from the bottom of the funnel.

All soil animals can also be extracted by mechanical washing methods, usually supplemented by flotation on salt solutions and sometimes by separation at the interface between liquids of different surface tension.

Many forms are destroyed by such methods which are also time-consuming and usually less satisfactory than methods depending on the animals' powers of mobility. But in some sands and deep agricultural clays and in the case of immobile animals mechanical methods are the only available ones.

For realistic results in productivity work the natural layer-structure of soil must be allowed for (e.g. the presence of litter, fermentation and humus layers). All soil animals are more or less restricted to certain layers and the depths of these vary from place to place.

3.1.2.3 *Catch-mark-recatch (CMR)*

If we capture, mark, and release at the same site the number a of individuals and later capture by the same method b individuals and find among them a' marked ones, the population numbers (N) in the area can be determined from the well-known equation of Lincoln:

$$N = b \cdot \frac{a}{a'} \quad \dots\dots\dots\dots\dots\dots\dots\dots\dots\dots\dots\dots\dots\dots\dots\dots\dots\dots\dots 3.1$$

This method gives unbiased results when: (1) the numbers (N) do not change significantly between sampling occasions (this calls for intervals between sampling to be as brief as possible), (2) the probability of capture after marking is the same for marked and unmarked individuals (the interval between sampling must be long enough for the two categories to mix adequately for random trapping), and (3) losses mortality and emigration are the same for marked and unmarked individuals. The application of Lincoln's method, to the census of mammals, even as modified by Leslie (1952) has been severely criticised by Hayne (1949), Tanton (1965) and others who maintain that it is to be recommended only when other methods are impracticable.

In other fields of ecology and especially in invertebrate studies CMR methods have been extensively developed and, bearing in mind the limitations mentioned, have proved most successful. In particular Jackson (1939, 1948) developed techniques of successive re-captures as a result of which the two components of population increase (birth versus immigration) can be distinguished from each other on the one hand and the two components of decrease (death and emigration) on the other. This method has been further developed by Glasgow (1953) and is explained by Andrewartha (1961) and by Dobson (1962). It depends on the use of a triangular matrix showing the proportions of the animals in the catch on each of a number of occasions which had previously been captured and the proportions which were subsequently re-captured. The totals summed along the sides of the triangle permit calculation of a positive series due to ingress of animals to the area under study and of a negative series due to egress from the area. This technique assumes constant rates of gain and loss throughout the period of sampling but the calculations are not difficult and it has provided valuable estimates not only in Jackson's own work on *Glossina* but also in that of Richards (1953) and Richards and Waloff (1954) on grasshoppers. The technique has been reviewed by Dobson (1962) and by Parr, Gaskell and George (1968).

A different matrix method was independently developed by Dowdeswell, Fisher and Ford (1940) and is further explained by Fisher and Ford (1947), Dowdeswell (1959) and by Parr, Gaskell and George (1968). Application is restricted to the particular case of a declining population and since no method of estimating standard errors of the population numbers has been developed, its use is very limited.

More recently, Jolly (1965) has described a method based on a stochastic model which demands that each individual should be given a unique mark. However, constant rates of gain and loss to the population are not assumed and both population size estimates and standard errors can be obtained.

In general, therefore, the mark-recapture methods have considerable application to the estimation of population size in invertebrate ecology in cases when any other procedure would be quite impracticable.

The catch-mark-recapture method can also be successfully used in small mammal studies in conjunction with the calendar of catches (Adams, 1959; Evans, 1949; Petrusewicz and Andrzejewski, 1962; Gliwicz *et al.*, 1968—see 3.1.2.1). The results of catches using CMR method, as calculated later from the calendar of catches (CC) supply substantial, additional information which is very important for the ecological analysis. It is possible to calculate the time of presence (t'_i), that is the time during which each individual remains in a given area, as well as the mean length of stay for an average individual (see Fig. 3.1):

$$\bar{t}' = 1/v \sum_{i=1}^{i=v} t_i$$

the discrete number of individuals (v), can be obtained by counting the captured animals; one can also calculate the exact trappability of each individual and the mean trappability for the whole population, or, for certain groups of individuals, e.g., males and females, trap-shy and trap-prone, young and old, those after the first, second, third . . . n-th catch, or those which were present in the study area for a definite number of days; the frequency of individuals from a different number of catches will allow us to distinguish groups of individuals with a different degree of trap-shyness or proneness as well as numbers within these groups. The number of newly caught and marked animals gives us an estimate of arrival (immigration and birth) and similarly the number of marked individuals which disappear from the records is a measure of disappearance due to emigration or mortality. From statistical calculations, it is possible to calculate the number of resident and migratory individuals (Wierzbowska and Petrusewicz, 1963), the increase in weight, etc. More details on possibilities opened up by this method can be found in Petrusewicz and Andrzejewski (1962), Gliwicz *et al.* (1968), Bujalska *et al.* (1968), Petrusewicz *et al.* (1968).

3.1.2.4 *Special methods*
There are numerous special methods for determining numbers depending

on the habits of the species considered. Only a few examples will be given below.

Varley determined successfully the numbers of winter moth by counting the larvae on their journey to the oak canopy, which is made only once by each individual, on a fixed number of tree trunks. The larvae that dropped from the canopy were counted again in randomly distributed catching trays.

An ingenious method was devised for *Carabidae* by Grüm (1969). He placed a number of pit-fall traps along both sides of a Carabidae-proof screen enclosing areas of 25–125 m². He marked the beetles trapped at the outside of the screen each with an individual number and released them inside the enclosure, the assumption being that they 'wanted to get in'. Those trapped at the inner side of the screen had their number, if any, read and recorded, and were thrown out of the enclosure, on the assumption that they 'wanted to get out'. After about a week there were only marked beetles within the enclosure. Grüm calculated their average numbers from the equation: $\bar{N} = v \cdot t'/_T$ (see equation 3.4), where $\bar{N}$ is the average numbers for the census period T in days, v is the number of individuals thrown into the enclosure, and $\bar{t}'$ is the average time, in days, during which individuals were present in the enclosure (duration of presence). In this way Grüm obtained not only the numbers (N) but also the rate of exchange of individuals in the census area.

To conclude this brief discussion of the principles of determining numbers (N) we may say: any method which affords an adequate reflexion of reality is useful.

3.1.3   Average numbers ($\bar{N}$) and number of individual-days ($\bar{N} \cdot T$)

For computing the elements of energy flow parameters (C, A, R, and FU) as well as for some methods of calculating production the knowledge of $\bar{N}$—average numbers during time period T—is essential. This is the precise quantity that defines the number of individuals responsible for consumption, respiration, reproduction, and so forth.

If the dynamic of a population is derived from 'k' censuses of numbers, then, *ex definitione:*

$$\bar{N} = 1/k \sum_{i=1}^{i=k} N_i \quad \dots\dots\dots\dots\dots\dots\dots\dots\dots\dots\dots\dots\dots\dots\dots 3.2$$

Note: average numbers thus calculated may incorporate a serious error if the censuses are irregularly spaced. Properly averaged numbers should be represented by weighted averages. Censuses taken at widely irregular intervals may give undue weight to accidentally low or high figures (Fig. 3.3). Hence, to calculate N̄ more accurately one may, after having plotted the population

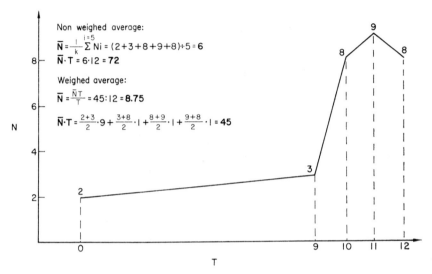

Figure 3.3. Average numbers (N) properly averaged.

dynamic curve; (1) divide the whole period of time into, say, ten or twenty regular intervals and calculate from the average, or better (2) calculate the area bounded by the curve (with a planimeter or from simple geometrical figures, usually trapezoids) and then divide it by time T.

In calculating various quantities relating to productivity we very often need the value N̄·T, which indicates the number of individual-days during time period T. For this is the quantity which is responsible for all the consumption, respiration, excretion, and elimination of metabolites, whilst the number of individual-days of pregnant females is the quantity directly responsible for the natural increase, i.e., all the new individuals born, hatched, etc. In these cases we may calculate N̄·T directly as the area bounded by the population dynamic curve, without calculating N̄ and then multiplying it by time T.

Although rarely in itself an object of study, the number of individual-days ($\bar{N} \cdot T$) is often essential for calculating many quantitites relating to productivity. For instance, in quantifying consumption we can multiply the daily consumption rate by the number of individual-days (see 5.2). One of the ways of calculating production is to multiply the average daily growth gain per individual by $\bar{N} \cdot T$ (see 4.4.1). The number of new individuals born during time T can be obtained by multiplying the daily birth rate per individual by the number of individual-days (see 4.2.1), and so forth.

When quantifying the various productivity concepts with the aid of individual-days ($\bar{N} \cdot T$) we must bear in mind that individuals are not all alike, that a young (small) individual may consume less in absolute terms than a fully grown one. Hence, knowledge of the over-all number of individual-days is usually not enough for productivity studies and we may need to measure that quantity with reference to definite age groups; we may often need to know the sex ratio, age structure, and the like. For instance, to calculate the number of new individuals produced (born or otherwise) over a certain period of time it is not enough to know over-all numbers ($\bar{N}$) of a population. We need the number of males ($N_{\male}$) and females ($N_{\female}$), and the number of pregnant females (N_p), since $\bar{N}_p \cdot T = \bar{N} \cdot s \cdot f \cdot T$, where $\bar{N}_p$ is the average number of gravid females during time T, $\bar{N}$ is the average number of individuals in the population, s is the sex ratio ($s = N^{\female}/N$), and f is the pregnancy ratio ($f = N_p/N$) (see 4.2.1).

Organisms in different age groups develop at different rates (have different growth gain—see 3.2). Consequently, if we wish to calculate production with the aid of daily growth rates (see 4.4) we must know numbers ($\bar{N}$) with reference to the various phases of individual development: developmental stages if any, age groups, or at least weight groups (assuming tacitly that animals within a single weight group have the same average daily rate of growth) (see 4.4.1).

3.1.4 Number of discrete individuals (v) present in a population during time T

In ecology, especially in productivity studies, we may want to know how many discrete individuals (v) occurred at any time during the period T or any fraction thereof. Neither instantaneous nor average numbers tell us anything about this. Average numbers, e.g., 10 individuals present during time T may mean 10 individuals present continuously throughout time T (their duration of presence t' equals T), or 20 individuals of which each was present for half of time T ($t' = T/2$), or 100 individuals of which each was present during one-tenth of time T ($t' = T/10$), or any other such combination. The number of discrete individuals which by living in a population for varying lengths of time make up its numbers is, as we mentioned above, something totally different from population numbers (N) and average numbers ($\bar{N}$). Only in a cohort, where all individuals are of the same age does $v = N$.

If in the course of time T there were in the population v discrete individuals, each of which was present in that population for t'_i days, then average time of presence should be, *ex definitione*:

$$t' = 1/v \cdot \sum_{i=1}^{i=v} t_i \dots\dots\dots\dots\dots\dots\dots\dots\dots 3.3$$

where

$$\sum_{i=1}^{i=v} t'_i$$

is the grand total of all the days spent by all the individuals in the population, i.e. the value of individual-days for time T. Hence

$$\sum_{i=1}^{i=v} t_i = v \cdot \bar{t}'$$

We have already shown (3.1.3) that the number of individual-days is also given by the quantity $\bar{N}$ T. Hence (Petrusewicz, 1966, 1967a):

$$v \cdot \bar{t}' = \bar{N} \cdot T \dots\dots\dots\dots\dots\dots\dots\dots\dots 3.4$$

and its derivatives, such as equation 1.10a ($v_T = NT/\bar{t}'$—see 1.2), which may be used for estimating the total number of discrete individuals occurring in the population during time period T, as well as for determining the number of individuals added to the population in the course of time T. Because $v = N_0 + v_r$ hence:

$$v_r = v - N_0 = \frac{\bar{N} \cdot T}{\bar{t}'} - N_0 \dots\dots\dots\dots\dots\dots\dots\dots\dots\dots\dots\dots\dots\dots\dots\dots 3.5$$

Note: v_r in equation 3·5 designates the number of new individuals born (hatched, eggs laid) in the population, the assumption being that there is no immigration. If immigration exists number of discrete individuals added to population is:

$$v_+ = v_r + v_{mg} = v - N_0 + v_{mg} \dots\dots\dots\dots\dots\dots\dots\dots\dots\dots\dots 3.6$$

When v is known, we can calculate $\bar{t}' = \bar{N} \cdot T/v$, or, by using Grüm's (1969) method, $\bar{N} = v \cdot \bar{t}'/_T$ (see 3.1.2.4).

It may be noted that $T/\bar{t}' = v/\bar{N}$ is the turnover rate (see 1.1, equation 1·9).

It should now be clear that numbers (N or $\bar{N}$) and the number of discrete individuals (v) which occurred in the population in the course of time T are completely different concepts*. Failure to distinguish between them is eventually bound to lead to confusion, whereas by keeping them apart we may give greater depth to our analyses and understanding of many ecological processes.

As an illustration we may consider cases of inverted pyramids of numbers, which are often obtained in quantitative studies of trophic relations. We are often inclined to attribute this inversion to mistakes and errors: either we suspect that the numbers of the organisms fed upon (producers) have been wrongly determined, or the higher trophic level (consumers) have some additional and different food source. Yet neither need be the case. If the organisms fed upon have a much higher turnover (i.e., a much shorter life

---

* When a cohort is considered, the numbers at the start (N_0) is the same as the number (v) of the discrete individuals present in it. The same applies to any fraction of the life time of the cohort: the initial numbers (N_0) at the beginning of that fraction is at the same time the number (v) of discrete individuals present in the cohort through the duration of the fraction of time considered, obviously with the proviso that there is no immigration.

time) than the consumers, they may be at any particular moment inferior in numbers to the latter (smaller numbers or biomass), but their production may be large enough to ensure both food for the consumer and continuing existence of the population.

Another example is the finding commonly made in studies concerning small mammals that the numbers (N) of young individuals (aged 1–3 weeks, 3–5 weeks, etc.) is, even in the breeding season, as a rule less than that of adults (see Fig. 3.4), all of which, after all, had been young at one time. Actually, the discrete number of young individuals, say at the age of 1–3 weeks (sucklings), is obviously much larger than that of adults, but the duration of their presence in the population is at the very outside three

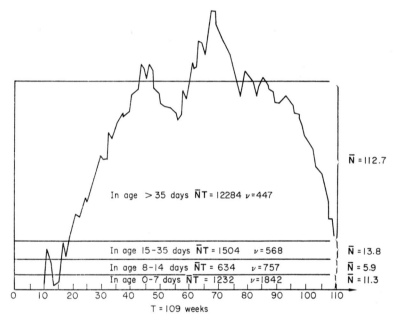

Figure 3.4. Dynamics of different age classes of white mouse population (data from Institute of Ecology, PAS).

The abundance of young, which are the most numerous class ($\nu_{(0-5)}=1842$ individuals) is very low (N=37) since their average life span is short ($t_{(0-5)}=1\cdot77$ weeks). The abundance of the older classes (more than 5 weeks old) is high ($\bar{N}=113$) though there are far fewer discrete individuals ($\nu_{(5-x)}=447$) whilst their life span is much longer ($t_{(5-x)}=26\cdot5$ weeks).

weeks, because after that time they pass into the next age group (upwards of three weeks). However average number ($\bar{N}$) depends on the average duration of presence in a population, because $\bar{N} = v \cdot \bar{t}'/T$ (equation 3·4), and this makes the numbers of young individuals very often smaller than that of adults.

When we consider the numbers of individuals by age groups we are led to the question and concept of the number of discrete individuals passing from one stage of development to the next, which is a quantity very useful for the determination of production (see 4.5). That particular number (v_s) can be calculated from the equation:

$$v_s = \bar{N}_s \cdot T/\bar{t}_s \dots\dots\dots 3.7$$

where $\bar{N}_s$ is the average numbers of the particular stage, and $\bar{t}_s$ is its average physiological duration. This equation is derived from equations 1·10 and 3·4. It is attractive in that it does not require the average duration of presence ($\bar{t}'$) to be estimated in the field, an operation which commonly poses very great difficulties. When we are given the average abundance of some stage ($\bar{N}_s$)—a quantity in any case essential in a great many ecological studies— and the duration of that stage, a physiological datum which usually varies within a narrow range, we are able to tell how many individuals have passed into the next stage within the time period considered. Provided it is possible to distinguish developmental stages and determine the numbers present at each stage survivorship curves can be constructed. By plotting survival curves we break down a population into cohorts, and—as will be shown below (see 4.3)—the production of a cohort is much more readily and accurately determined than that of a population of continuously reproducing animals (for examples of such procedure see chapter 4.5).

Another use to which we may turn the concept of the number of discrete individuals (v) with reference to a population and the time of measurement is for determining the number of individuals eliminated (v_E) in the course of time T. If we are given the average ecological longevity ($\bar{t}$), then:

$$v_E = \bar{N} \cdot T/\bar{t} \dots\dots\dots 3.8$$

To sum up, we may repeat that v, which stands for the number of discrete individuals present in a population during the time of measurement T, represents a notion completely different from that of numbers N. The former is a quantity that accumulates with the passage of time: it is legitimate to add up the several values of number (v_E) of animals actually eliminated—or (v_+) actually added to the population—in the course of particular fractions of time T. But adding up numbers (N) leads us nowhere. The number of discrete individuals present in a population, together with the durations of their presence, determines numbers N. We have indicated the following equations:

(1) the number of discrete individuals present which occurred at any time in the population during period T:

$$v = \bar{N} \cdot T / \bar{t}' \text{ (} \bar{t}' \text{ being the average duration of presence)} \dots \dots \dots (3.4)$$

(2) the number of individuals born in the course of time T:

$$v_r = v_T - N_0 = \bar{N} \cdot T / \bar{t}' - N_0 \dots \dots \dots \dots \dots \dots \dots \dots \dots \dots (3.5)$$

(3) the discrete number of individuals added to the population during the time period T:

$$v_+ = v_r + v_{mg} = \bar{N} T / \bar{t}' - N_0 + v_{mg} \dots \dots \dots \dots \dots \dots \dots \dots (3.6)$$

(4) the number of individuals eliminated during time T:

$$v_E = \bar{N} \cdot T / \bar{t} \text{ (} \bar{t} \text{ being the average ecological longevity)} \dots \dots \dots (3.8)$$

(5) the number of individuals that have passed into the next stage (production of a stage, the starting figure of the survivorship curve of the next stage):

$$v_s = \bar{N}_s \cdot T / \bar{t}_s \text{ (} \bar{t}_s \text{ being the duration of stage s)} \dots \dots \dots \dots \dots \dots (3.7)$$

3.2 Weight and biomass

3.2.1 Measurement of weight

For estimating production (P) as well as energy flow and the associated quantities (C, A, R, FU) it is essential to know weight (W) and weight gain (ΔW) and hence rate of weight gain $\Delta W/t$. Individual weight will be obtained by weighing a representative number of individuals and calculating the average. Individuals should be chosen to represent either age classes or a succession of known time intervals in the history of their population. Although it is usually easy with captive animals, the weighing procedure nevertheless calls for a few observations.

(1) When the weight of small meso- and micro-fauna is to be determined it is necessary to appraise the relative advantages of direct weighing and of more indirect methods in the light of the animals in question and of available equipment. Arthropods such as small beetles, woodlice etc. weighing tens of milligrams can easily be weighed on a conventional chemical balance provided the operation is performed quickly enough to avoid evaporation. If animals such as aphids and larger collembola (weighing about 0·1 mg to a few milligrams) are to be weighed accurately on such a balance, a number must usually be weighed together and it is thus not possible to follow the weight changes of individuals. Below this level of sensitivity two types of microbalance are particularly useful and both have sensitivities well below a microgramme. Torsion balances can be bought commercially (at about $300–$1000) or can be constructed by the experimenter using quartz fibres or the 'hair spring' of a watch. Electromicrobalances use the principle of suspending the weight from the needle of a moving-coil micro-ampere meter and restoring the needle to its zero position by passing a measured current. These, too, can be made by hand or bought from makers such as Cahn (U.K.) Ltd., 27 Essex Road, Dartford, Kent, and Research and Industrial Instrument Co., 17 Stannery Street, London, S.E.11.

Different models vary in range, speed of weighing and sensitivity but the electromicrobalances, and especially that due to Research and Industrial Inst. Co. permit rapid and accurate weighing of small mites, collembola etc. without dessication.

In many cases the trouble and expense of direct weighing is not justified, and recourse may be had to linear measurements which are converted to weights by means of a regression formula. In some cases width and length have been incorporated in the formula and in others length only: examples being:

$$W = a(1+k), \text{ or } W = b.l^c, \text{ or } W = bl^c L^d, \text{ or } W^1 = b.l^c, \text{ or } W^1 = b.W^c$$

Where W = fresh weight
$\quad W^1$ = dry weight
$\quad l$ = length
$\quad L$ = width

a, b, c, d, k are constants for a particular species or group of species, which must be determined empirically. Selected examples are listed in Table 3.1; examples of the extensive use of this approach are the work of Berthet (1964) for mites and for Nematoda by Nielsen (1949). Another indirect method, suitable for small animals is the chemical determination of nitrogen by Kjeldahl analysis and determination of a constant by which to relate this to biomass. The method was used for marine animals by Zeuthen (1947) and has the advantage that it is a more realistic estimate of protoplasm than is weight in the case of animals with heavy exoskeletons or shells. In spite of these improvements in the determination of weight of small organisms, further technical progress is particularly to be desired in the case of very small animals such as Nematoda and Protozoa.

TABLE 3.1. Calculation of weight of animals from linear measurements. W – fresh weight, W' – dry weight, l – length, L – width of animals.

Species	Formula	References
Daphnia	$W = 0.052\, l^{3.0}$	Winberg *et al.* (1968)
Bosmina	$W = 0.124\, l^{2.2}$	Winberg *et al.* (1968)
Diaphanosoma	$W = 0.092\, l^{2.4}$	Winberg (1968)
Araneus 1st group	$W = 6.14\, l + 13.14$	Kajak A. (unpublish.)
2nd group	$W = 6.37\, l - 15.42$	Kajak A. (unpublish.)
Trochosa ruricola	$W' = 0.275\, l^{1.98}$	Breymeyer A. (1967a)
Trochosa ruricola	$W' = 0.444\, W^{0.94}$	Breymeyer A. (1967a)
Trochosa ruricola	$W' = 5.08\, l - 21.20$	Breymeyer A. (1967b)
Various spiders	$W' = 0.429\, W^{0.86}$	Breymeyer A. (1967b)
Oribatei	$W = l^{1.58}.L^{1.45}.10^{6.61}$	Berthet (1967)
Isopoda	$W' = 1.56\, W - 1.24$	Breymeyer and Brzozowska (in litt.)

(2) Difficulties of a completely different kind may be encountered in weighing large animals. Milner (1967) reports that stomach contents may be up to 15 per cent of the weight of animals which, in addition, drink between 5 to 70 kg of water. Weighing together with such large amounts of food and water may lead to significantly wrong results. Preferably, weighing hours should be fixed for a particular category of animals according to their habits. In cattle, for instance, day-to-day variations are less when weighing is done 3–4 hours after sunrise. Actually this problem is encountered in virtually all research concerned with weight, only the differences may not be so striking. Walkowa has found food to account for about 0.6 g $\pm$ 0.023 per average individual (20–25 g) of white mice.

3.2.2 Individual growth and rate of weight gain

In productivity studies it is often essential to know the weight gain of an organism and to plot an individual growth curve. The difficulties that may be involved in determinations of weight, some of which have been referred to in the preceding section (3.2.1), are here obviously the same but are further compounded by an even greater problem—that of finding animals of known age. This is no great obstacle with animals bred in captivity but growth curves recorded under laboratory conditions are often apt to lead one astray when applied to field populations. For instance, an individual growth curve plotted (Drożdż, 1965) for *Clethrionomys glareolus* bred under laboratory conditions gave the weight of 7 g at the age of 12 days, when the animal is still blind. Yet in the field it is not at all uncommon to find this weight in animals which are already fully independent members of a population (Bujalska and Gliwicz, 1968). Hence, laboratory data on growth and rate of weight gain must be applied very cautiously to field conditions.

When an individual growth curve is to be plotted the following procedures may be followed.

(1) When studying a cohort, we are dealing with individuals of the same or almost the same age. Here the weight determined at definite intervals is automatically the weight for a particular age. By plotting it on the y-axis against the time of measurement T—which here is to all practical purposes equivalent to the age of the animal—we obtain readily the individual growth curve.

We are quite frequently concerned with cohorts, and various cases are discussed in section 4.3. Usually though, we are dealing with populations where different generations overlap. This compels us to use different methods.

(2) The age of some animals can be determined from certain morphological and physiological indices, such as the wear of teeth in rodents and large grazing animals, the weight of the eye lens in rodents, ossification of cartilaginous parts, e.g., pelvic and cranial bones, etc. Here the situation is relatively simple. A sufficiently large number of animals has to be trapped, and their weight and age determined. It should be stressed that it is essential to have the absolute age, the age from the moment of birth; even the largest series showing successive ossification, or increase in the weight of the eye lens, is useless in productivity studies unless it is referred to age. Then, by plotting weight against age we obtain the individual growth curve.

In many animals, especially among invertebrates, it is possible to distinguish different life stages: eggs, consecutive larval instars, pupae, imagines, and the like, and also to determine the duration of these stages. The average weight for the different stages is then plotted on the y-axis against the mid-point of their duration on the x-axis, and the plots are connected by straight lines, or by 'idealized' probable curves.

Two methods of plotting curves—not only of growth—from meagre data, are commonly suggested: Some people always prefer to draw straight lines between the points, which in their view makes for the lesser error. Others favour a 'smoothing' of the curves and drawing of the 'probable' flexures of 'ideal curves', which they argue are closer to reality. Reality is probably better reflected by the 'smoothed' curves, but firstly it is not possible to determine how much closer to truth such a curve is, when compared to a straight line, and secondly there is always some risk that the error is even greater than with the straight line and there is usually no means of measuring the risk. It therefore seems that, additional data wanting, the safer and more objective way is to use straight lines.

As yet, however, we are able to determine age for relatively few species, and the methods are also very imperfect, the information gathered with their aid being indicative of rather broad classes of age only. Progress is badly needed in this field.

(3) Another way is to capture and mark individually as large a number as possible of individuals of known age, for instance, very young ones, in which case possible errors are in terms of days rather than weeks. Their weight on recapture together with age determined from records will enable us to plot an individual growth curve.

(4) If, for some reason or other, an individual growth curve for the species investigated is not available, a rough and ready but much used method is to apply the growth curve of a species related as closely as possible, to the former; in this case it is necessary to know the weight at one well established age at least. Assuming that the two curves are similar in shape—as they often are—the shape of the known one is used to construct the other, after due consideration of the weight ratio between the two species as indicated by their weights at the known age of both.

The literature relating to individual growth is already profuse. Much of it is devoted to an analysis of its pattern in time, its rate and other aspects. Growth curves are already known for most domestic and laboratory animals as well as for over fifty species of wild animals, some of them plotted from laboratory data. There is also some comfort to be derived from the fact that growth being a physiological and obligatory process, the curves are not so variable as are ecological data relating to numbers, natality, mortality, etc. Hence, when a growth curve has been prepared once, it may be also used for the particular species under altered conditions without fear of a major mistake—except in the case of such extreme changes as those between laboratory and field conditions. In productivity studies the growth curve is merely a means and not the objective of the study. Therefore, we shall not discuss these interesting questions further but will refer those interested in them to the work of Brody (1945), Simpson, Roe, and Lewontinz (1960), Bertalanffy (1957a), Winberg (1966), and Welty (1962). Let us only mention that—as is widely accepted—most species have the same basic sigmoid shape of growth curve in common. In any concrete case, however, this shape may be very peculiarly expressed, as may be seen from the example of *Tribolium castaneum* (Fig. 3.5), for which the individual growth curve has been plotted with great precision on the basis of the extensive material of Klekowski *et al.* (1967). Some known individual growth curves are given for the sake of example (Fig. 3.5).

The factors most commonly referred to as affecting rate of growth are the abundance and availability of food, density of the population, and temperature.

Besides the individual growth curve, another parameter which may be a subject of independent research and is often essential for calculating production is the rate of weight gain. Here distinction is made between the finite, e.g., daily weight gain, and instantaneous weight gain.

3.2.2.1 *Average daily weight gain*

When the individual growth curve has been obtained, we can readily find the weight gained $\Delta W = W_2 - W_1$ by an individual between instants in the organism's life t_1 and t_2 (Fig. 3.6). The time during which the weight gain takes place is usually measured in days, and when the latter are divided into the former we obtain the absolute daily weight gain (ADWG) per average, or statistical individual:

$$v = \frac{W_2 - W_1}{t_2 - t_1} = \Delta W / \Delta t \dots\dots\dots\dots\dots\dots\dots\dots\dots\dots\dots\dots 3.9$$

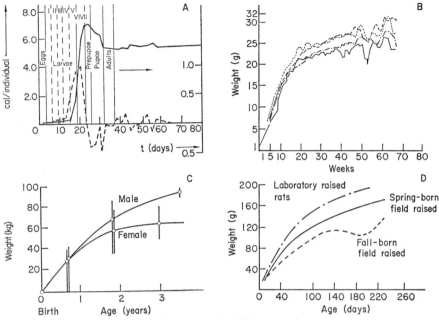

Figure 3.5. Examples of individual growth curves.

A. Calorific value (continuous line) and absolute 24 hour growth (dotted line) of one individual of *Tribolium castaneum* (from Klekowski *et al.* 1967).

B. Individual growth curves of four populations of white mice (from Walkowa and Petrusewicz, 1967).

C. Growth curve for Uganda Kob from fresh carcass weight and estimated age. Vertical line represents the range in observed weights (from Buechner and Golley, 1967).

D. Comparison of growth of rats in field and laboratory (from Golley, 1967).

We may also want to know the growth rate per unit weight of an organism, which is the relative daily weight gain rate (RDWG) and is calculated by dividing the absolute daily growth by the average weight of an organism:

$$v' = \frac{(W_2 - W_1) \cdot 2}{(t_2 - t_1) \cdot (W_2 + W_1)} = \frac{\Delta W}{\Delta t \cdot \overline{W}} \dots\dots\dots\dots\dots\dots\dots\dots\dots 3.10$$

When the whole individual growth curve is divided into sections according to time, it is possible to determine the growth gain at particular moments of an individual's life. By plotting these values on the y-axis against the mid

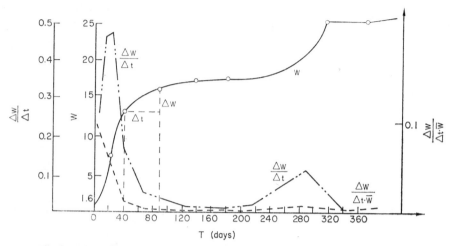

Figure 3.6. Individual growth (W), absolute growth rate ($\triangle W/\triangle t$) and relative rate of weight gain ($\triangle W/\triangle t.\bar{W}$) curves of *Clethrionomys glareolus* (data from Bujalska *et al.*, 1968).

time intervals for which the average weight gains rates have been calculated it is possible to construct a curve of weight gain.

Note: the time intervals for which we determine the average weight gain (absolute or relative) in order to construct the growth gain curve need not be evenly spaced in the individual's life time; but care should be exercised that the individual growth curve sections corresponding to them be as nearly rectilinear as possible. It is advisable to perform these operations on large-scale graphs.

3.2.2.2 *Instantaneous weight gain rate*
Although it is a very useful quantity, the use of an average daily weight gain assumes a linear gain of growth, which is certainly not justifiable throughout a long span of life. Brody (1945) gives a characteristic example: a cow weighing 1000 lbs, 1000 days after conception will have an average absolute daily weight gain rate $v = 1$ lb/day. Yet there will be only very few days, perhaps none at all, on which the actual weight increment is 1 lb. One week after conception v is 0·0001 lb, at the age of five months 4 lbs, and at the age of 1000 days 0·25 lb per day.

Obviously, the shorter the time interval under consideration the less variation there will be among absolute daily weight gains, and the closer they will be to the actual (instantaneous) weight gains or, to put it differently, the closer will be the average daily weight gain calculated for that time interval to actual weight gains. Hence it may be readily understood why there is among ecologists a tendency to seek not only a finite absolute (or relative) weight gain but also the true instantaneous absolute (or relative) weight gain, which is the weight increment during an infinitely short time interval, and is expressed by the differential

$$q = \frac{dw/dt}{W}$$

Obviously it is not possible to measure 'dw'—the instantaneous weight increment—either in the field or even in the laboratory. But here the ecologist is rescued by the mathematician, who solves this problem for him with the aid of complicated mathematical operations—which the ecologist need not necessarily understand and on the basis of certain assumptions, which the ecologist must know and be able to justify. One assumption is that q is constant, which means that rate of weight gain is exponential in character. If not always true, this assumption can usually be accepted by an ecologist. By solving differential equation $dw/dt = qWt$ we obtain then

$$\int_{W_0}^{Wt} dw/dt = q \int_0^t dt$$

and integration of the exponential function gives us:

$$W_t = W_0 . e^{q.(t_2 - t_1)} \quad \dots\dots\dots\dots\dots\dots\dots\dots\dots\dots\dots 3.11$$

and hence:

$$q = (\ln Wt_2 - \ln Wt_1) : (t_2 - t_1) \dots\dots\dots\dots\dots\dots\dots 3.12$$

Instantaneous relative rate of weight gain (instantaneous growth rate in terms of weight) has many uses in ecology, including the calculation of production (for which see 4.4.2).

As has already been said, the shape of the individual growth curve is usually sigmoid. The curves of individual rate of weight gain (absolute as well as relative), on the other hand, reach a peak at young age (Figs. 3.6 and 3.5A) and then fall to zero level in animals attaining maximum development at a certain age, or continue at a low level for continuously growing animals, such as certain reptiles and fishes. It is not uncommon to see it fall below zero, for instance for pupal instars, for many arthropods immediately after hatching, or during hibernation or aestivation, for many mammals in the rut period, and the like.

In productivity studies weight or biomass gain, may be defined in terms of live (or fresh, or wet) or dead weight—these being usually taken to be the same—or dry weight, or ash-free (organic matter) weight, or energy content (calorific value), the last-named indicating the amount of heat—in calories—obtained by complete combustion of organic matter (see section 5.2). The units that lend themselves best for comparison are calories.

3.2.3 Biomass

The total mass of living organisms present in a population or in any arbitrary ecological unit at a given time moment in unit space is referred to as biomass or standing crop.

Biomass can either be measured by adding up the weights of all animals, which for this purpose all need to be captured and weighed, or calculated by multiplying the average individual weight obtained at a census by numbers (N).

The accuracy of estimates depends principally on the accuracy of determinations of numbers (see 3.1.2) and of weighing (see 3.2.1).

Changes in the biomass are the resultant of individual growth, reproduction, mortality, immigration, and emigration. As has already been said, they tell us little, if anything, about production. Only in some not very common situations, for instance, during the rather brief period of rapid development after winter, when mortality is fairly low, is production quite closely reflected in biomass growth.

But at any specified moment the standing crop is what is responsible for all assimilation and respiration. The same may be said of the quantity $\bar{B} \cdot T$, which we may agree to call 'biomass-day'. Hence the quantities $\bar{B}$ and $\bar{B} \cdot T$ are required in certain estimates of energy flow parameters (see section 6.4) and certain methods of calculating production (see section 4.4).

The statement that the standing crop is the quantity responsible for the accumulation and dissipation of energy (assimilation and respiration) calls for some qualification. It is obviously the individual organisms that consume, breathe, etc. A bigger individual consumes and assimilates more than a small one, but this is not a simple linear relation. Respiration and assimilation will be much larger for four mice each weighing 7 g than for one individual weighing 28 g (see section 6.2.3). This explains why it is so important to have not only the total, overall biomass for the population, but also its distribution among individual age or weight groups.

3.2.4 Energy: calorific determinations

In order to be able to compare such different organic matter as, e.g., faeces, body and milk, we must convert the different components of feeding and productivity equations into a common currency and it is necessary to determine their calorific values by combustion. Formerly wet combustion methods, using acids, were employed (Ivlev, 1934) but the availability of accurate and relatively simple bomb calorimeters has resulted in their widespread use today. In this section these methods and a range of calorific values are presented.

In principle the determination of calorific values of combustible organic material is simple. The material is first dried in such a way as to avoid chemical and microbial decomposition. This may be performed in a drying chamber at a temperature of 104°C or lower, in a vacuum oven at 60°C or by freeze drying: each technique has its proponents and the relative efficiencies of different methods have not been properly compared, but it is certain that normal drying methods can bring about serious reductions of calorific value (e.g. Komor, 1940). Next the material is ground, for instance in a hammer mill, homogenised and compressed into pellets.

Calorimeters can be of the adiabatic type in which the temperature of the surrounding container is made to rise with that of the calorimeter. This prevents heat losses and permits direct calculation of the heat generated from the temperature rise and the thermal capacity of the calorimeter. This type of calorimeter is widely available commercially and is suitable for the combustion of fairly large samples of the order of a gramme or more. It has been used to determine the calorific value of mammalian tissues, faeces, food etc.

A somewhat similar machine in a miniature version was described by

Slobodkin and Richman (1960). This was a unique instrument, expensive and demanding skilled operation, largely on account of the need to match, manually, the temperature rise in bomb with that in the surrounding water-bath.

An alternative principle is that of the ballistic calorimeter (Fig. 3.7) in which the temperature rise of an insulated bomb is related empirically to the calorific value of known charges, usually of benzoic acid, which can be bought with a certified calorific value in the region of 6·324 kcal/g. Earlier micro-bombs of this type (e.g. Calvet and Prat, 1963) tended to be somewhat elaborate but Phillipson (1964) has developed one based on a spherical chamber, permitting lighter construction and a low thermal capacity (Fig. 3.8). This is now available commercially from the Wiegert-Gentry Instrument Company, Aiken, South Carolina, U.S.A.

The main sources of error in bomb calorimetry, and especially in very small bombs, are due to incomplete combustion. This is largely overcome

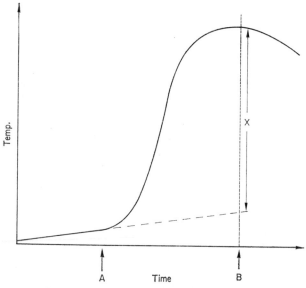

Figure 3.7. Temperature curve of an empirically calibrated ballistic bomb calorimeter: Abscissa=time, A=time of firing, B=time of maximum temperature, Ordinate=temperature, x=temperature rise.

The initial temperature rise is allowed to stabilize until it can be extrapolated in order to permit reliable measurement of x.

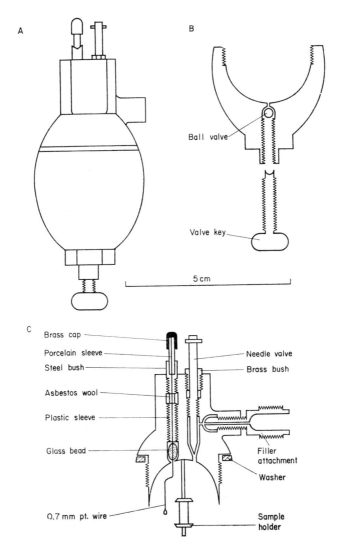

A

B

Ball valve

Valve key

5 cm

C

Brass cap

Porcelain sleeve

Steel bush

Asbestos wool

Plastic sleeve

Glass bead

0.7 mm pt. wire

Needle valve

Brass bush

Filler attachment

Washer

Sample holder

Figure 3.8. Diagram of calorific bomb (after Phillipson).

A. Assembled except for air jackets.
B and C. Details of construction.

by the use of high oxygen pressures—of the order of 30 atmospheres. With the same objective the addition of Benzoic acid to the biological material in order to maintain a minimum charge and ensure complete combustion has been advocated as also has the lining of the chamber with a thermal insulator such as alumina (Calvet and Prat). Certain subsidiary chemical reactions such as the endothermic breakdown of carbonates and reactions with nitrogen from the air are also potential sources of error (Southwood, 1966, Chapter 14).

A considerable range of calorific values of biological materials has now been published, the major sources being Golley (1961), Westlake (1963),

TABLE 3.2. Energy values of some types of organic matter cal/g dry wt.

Type of organic matter		Energy value (cal/g dry wt)	Reference
Average of 57 plants species	Leaves	4229	Golley (1961)
	Stems	4267	
	Roots	4720	
	Seeds	5965	
Average of dominant vegetation	*Spartinia*	4072	
	Poa old-field	4075	
	Pinus stand	4787	
	Alpine meadow	4711	
	Tundra	4709	
Antropogon virginicus old field	Green grass	4373	
	Standing dead	4290	
	Roots	4167	
	Litter	4139	
	Green herbs	4288	
	Average	4251	
Crustacea	*Daphnia*	4419	
	Stenona	5596	
	Uca and other crabs	2248	
Mollusca	*Modiolus*	4600	
Annelida		4617	
Mammalia	*Apodemus flavicollis* winter	4369	
	summer	5361	Górecki (1967)
	autumn	5274	
	Clethrionomys glareolus winter	4472	
	summer	5171	
	autumn	5161	

Wiegert (1964), Comita and Schindler (1963) and a selection of values given by the first of these authors is presented in Table 3.2; it will be observed that values within each group cover a considerable range, presumably due to environmental, seasonal and life cycle factors. Thus Wiegert (1964) obtained the following values for the egg, larva, male and female respectively of *Philaenus spumarius:* 6,300, 5,300, 5,700, 5,900 and Southwood (1966) quotes, 5,000 and 6,300 for the adult and the larva respectively of *Tenebrio molitor.*

Clearly the ecologist can legitimately use calorific values at two levels: firstly in the study of a particular species, in which case detailed measurements under the condition of the study are essential; and secondly in a more extensive synthesis involving comparisons between species and ecosystems. In the latter case approximate figures such as those in Table 3.2 can be used as conversion factors from food weights. This approach is further justified by the discovery of Slobodkin and Richman (1961), who pointed out that the *fat free* calorific value of dry animal tissues is surprisingly uniform and tends to lie between 5,400 and 6,100 calories per g. Higher values indicate animals which are unusually well fed or contain storage materials for eggs; these could be estimated by a simple fat extraction and calorific estimates could thus be arrived at without resort to bomb calorimetry. Very low figures in Table 3.2 are clearly those corresponding to animals with heavy inert exoskeletons. In such cases an index of protein content (such as Kjeldahl nitrogen) might be more usefully correlated with calorific content as was used by Zeuthen (1947) as a basis for comparisons of metabolic activity.

3.3 Longevity, survival, and other important parameters

3.3.1 Time in ecological research

In ecological research we are likely to deal with the following concepts of time.

(1) Time moment, for instance the moment at which a sample is taken or a census made; it will be designated T_1, T_2, T_3 . . . T_i.

(2) Time interval, for instance, time period of investigation, the intervals between censuses, the time of measurement, the duration of the breeding season or of the season of the year, or other such absolute units of time. They will be designated by T, or, if the need arises to distinguish more than one such time interval, T_I, T_{II}, etc.

(3) Lifetime of an organism, which will be designated by t.

When considering the lifetime of organisms we may have to distinguish among the following different concepts.

(3.1) Ecological longevity t—as the time during which an individual lives in a particular ecosystem. An ecologist is obviously little concerned with the longevity of any one individual; his interest lies with the average individual (or statistical) longevity ($\bar{t}$) in a definite population under specified conditions, which is *ex definitione* given by the equation:

$$\bar{t} = 1/v \sum_{i=1}^{i=v} t_i \dots\dots\dots\dots\dots\dots\dots\dots\dots\dots\dots\dots\dots\dots\dots 3.13$$

(3.2) Average duration of presence (t′) of an individual in the population within the measurement time period T.

(3.3) The duration of some stage in an organism's life cycle—t_s; this may be the time of development of the egg (t_e), the time of pregnancy (t_p), the duration of a larval instar, and the like.

Each of the concepts distinguished here may have some different use in ecological analysis and calculations of various quantities relating to productivity. Very important is the average longevity ($\bar{t}$), strictly speaking the average ecological longevity. It is highly variable because it depends very much on the sum total of the ecological conditions under which the population exists. As a very general index it has its shortcomings and advantages. One of the advantages is that it reflects the totality of the ecological conditions, or rather the total effect of this on the population. Among its shortcomings is the fact that it is a very general index, which affords no clue as to why longevity is at a particular level in the investigated population.

As has already been said (section 3.1.4), when the average ecological longevity is given we are able to determine the number of individuals eliminated during time T from the equation (3.8) $v_E = \bar{N}T/\bar{t}$. The reciprocal of longevity is the index of mortality ($\mu = 1/\bar{t}$). The index $T/\bar{t}$ is the turnover of individuals, which tells us how large a part of the average numbers of the population has been exchanged during time T. In field work, $\bar{t}$ is only relatively easy to obtain for the cohort, because the survivorship curve shows us how many individuals are still alive at any definite moment. Where we are unable to distinguish cohorts the ecological longevity can be arrived at empirically only in exceptional cases (cf. individual growth curve—section 3.3.2).

The average duration of presence in a population—t′—during time T is a quantity that has been forced upon the researcher by his choice of the time

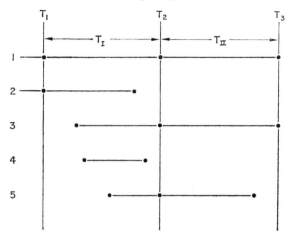

Figure 3.9. The effect of time period of investigation on the time of presence (t′).

The diagram illustrates the time of presence of an individual in population (t′) during time T. Dots represent initial and final points of the recorded time of presence. In the case when the individual lived before T_1 or after T_2, the duration of presence is not a biological measurement but is imposed by the observer. Duration of presence for those individuals which lived beyond T_2 (individuals 1, 3 and 5) will be different in the case of time T_1–T_2 as compared with T_1–T_3, and thus depends on observation. The sum of durations of presence is the number of individual-days $\bar{N}{\cdot}T$.

period of investigation—T, or rather by the necessity of confining his considerations to any such period (Fig. 3.9). For individuals which were also alive before time moment T_1 (see Fig. 3.9) or have survived beyond time T_2, it is not a significant biological characteristic. For instance the individuals 3 and 4 in Fig. 3.9 may have been new born individuals or immigrants of unknown age. Furthermore, the size of the censused area is not without influence on the calculated duration of presence. When the area chosen is unduly small as compared with the motility of the organisms the estimate of duration in the population will be too low owing to abnormally high levels of 'immigration' and 'emigration', which would in fact be nothing but the natural movement of the individuals within their normal home ranges. Nevertheless, the quantity $\bar{t}'$ may not infrequently be useful in a variety of calculations involving, for instance, equation 3.4 – $v{\cdot}\bar{t}' = \bar{N}{\cdot}T$, where v is the number of discrete individuals which for some fraction of time T were part of the population considered (see 3.1.4).

The physiological longevity, or the duration of some stage in the life cycle, is usually not difficult to estimate and is often of help in calculations relating to productivity. For instance, it enables us to estimate the number of individuals passing at some definite moment of time into the next stage in their life (equation 3·7; $v_s = \bar{N} \cdot T / t_s$) and then to plot the approximate survivorship curve and estimate production with reasonable accuracy (see section 4.5).

3.3.2 Survivorship curve and mortality

The survivorship curve is the starting point for many ecological analyses. This is a graph showing the number of organisms still alive at some definite moment (Fig. 3.10). The graph is rather easily prepared for a cohort: in which case the population dynamic curve is the same as the survivorship curve.

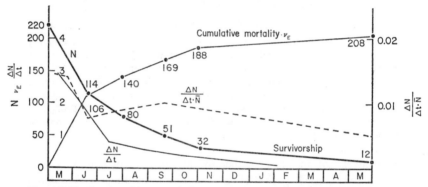

Figure 3.10. Survivorship, cumulative mortality and mortality curves (data from Gliwicz *et al.*, 1967).

The survivorship curve indicates how many individuals have lived up to a given individual age (t). Cumulative mortality shows how many of the population have perished up to the given time.

Absolute mortality rate curves illustrate how many of the population disappeared daily on the average ($\Delta N / \Delta t$). This rate of disappearance is plotted against the mid-point of the time period Δt. The mortality rate curve or relative mortality rate, shows how many individuals on average disappeared daily per one individual ($\Delta N / \Delta t \bar{N}$). Value of mortality rate is plotted against mid-point of time period $\Delta t = t_2 - t_1$.

Where populations with overlapping generations are concerned—the vast majority of cases—the situation is far more difficult and survivorship curves can be plotted only under one of the following two circumstances.

1   We must be able to determine the age structure of the standing crop at consecutive censuses; an analysis of the numerical size of age groups may tell us how many individuals of the population considered have reached a definite age. The difficulties here are great because it is only occasionally that we are able to determine age accurately (see 3.2.2) and, furthermore, the age-structure is not infrequently so upset by immigration and emigration that survivorship figures are often altogether unrealistic.

2   We must be able to distinguish the different stages of the life cycle of the organisms investigated and know their physiological duration time t_s (see section 4.5).

The survivorship curve provides a starting point for many important statistics, such as the following.

(1) The specific cumulative mortality curve, which tells us how many organisms have died up to a definite moment of time. It is constructed by plotting the values N_0-N_T found from the survivorship curve against the corresponding time moments T_i (see Fig. 3.10).

(2) The specific mortality of individuals of a population, that is, the number of organisms eliminated during a definite time interval of their life: $(N_1 - N_2):(t_2 - t_1)$. We can prepare the curve of this mortality by plotting the value $(N_1 - N_2):(t_2 - t_1)$ etc. against the mid point of the corresponding time intervals $t_2 - t_1$ (see Fig. 3.10).

(3) The specific daily mortality rate, or mortality. This is the number of individuals eliminated per unit life time interval per individual:

$$m = \frac{N_1 - N_2}{\frac{N_1 + N_2}{2} \cdot (t_2 - t_1)} = \frac{\Delta N}{\Delta t \cdot \bar{N}} \quad \dots \dots \dots \dots \dots \dots \dots \dots \dots \dots \dots \dots \quad 3.14$$

or, for a very brief time interval $\Delta N/\Delta t \cdot N_0$. When survivorship is represented by an exponential or nearly exponential curve the mortality rate is constant.

The daily mortality rate is an average value, statistically correct for the time interval considered, but it is not valid for particular moments in time. As in the case of growth rate (see 3.2.2), we may be interested to know the true, instantaneous mortality rate. When the survivorship curve is exponential (this has to be checked, e.g., by the chi-square method) we calculate the instantaneous mortality rate by pulling the equation $N_T = N_0 \cdot e^{-\mu t}$ into the logarithmic form, which yields:

$$\eta = \frac{\ln N_0 - \ln N_t}{t} \quad \dots\dots\dots\dots\dots\dots\dots\dots\dots\dots\dots\dots\dots\dots \quad 3.15$$

When the survivorship curve departs from the exponential, equation 3.15 can be used to calculate the instantaneous mortality rate only for short sections of the survivorship curve, on the assumption that for brief intervals of time the curve does not differ from an exponential one.

4

Measurement of Production

4.1 General principles

Measurement of production by an individual animal involves no special difficulties: the difference in the animal's weight between two arbitrarily selected times is the production over the included period. Quantification of population production on the other hand is exceptionally difficult. The production value is the product of individual growth (development plus deposition of fat), natality and mortality, all of which processes occur simultaneously. Furthermore, production includes organic matter incorporated in their bodies by those animals which have been eliminated from the population (by death, predation and emigration). When it is also remembered that body growth is a continual process, the resulant of assimilation, the difficulties of measuring population production accurately will be appreciated.

To obtain an empirical estimate of production it is necessary to know the number and weight (or energy content) of all eliminated animals at the time of elimination, the energy content of hair, faeces, dead skin, moult and similar products, together with the body-weight gains of all survivors and of all immigrants (from the moment of their joining the population). All this is an impossible task even in the case of laboratory populations and it follows that population production (P) cannot be measured directly, but only calculated with the aid of various assumptions and simplifications.

The process of organic matter (or energy) accumulation can be approached from two entirely different, but not contrary viewpoints. Firstly, production, which is a result of nutrition, is that portion of assimilated matter which was not used in maintenance which can be expressed as derivatives of formulae 1.2 and 1.3 as follows:

$$P = A - R \dotfill 4.1$$
$$P = C - (FU + R) \dotfill 4.2$$

Secondly, population production may occur through reproduction; i.e. production of new individuals (P_r) and also through bodily growth of individuals already present in the population (P_g). Hence:

$$P = P_r + P_g \dots\dots\dots\dots\dots\dots\dots\dots\dots\dots\dots\dots\dots\dots\dots\dots 4.3$$

We can therefore calculate production which is due to reproduction (P_r) or that which is due to growth (P_g) or total production (P).

Methods used for quantification of population production (P) depend on the ecological properties and behaviour of the group investigated, on the habitat, the sophistication of methods for gathering empirical data and accessibility of these methods, the availability of technical equipment and—and this is very important—on the amount of time that can be devoted to field investigation. Hence the variety of methods is so great, that it would not be an exaggeration to say, that almost every scientist measures population production by somewhat different means. We do not undertake to present here all possible ways of calculating population production (P). We will only try to indicate various principles.

It would appear that the easiest way to define the magnitude of production would be to calculate it on the basis of the above mentioned formulae 4.1 and 4.2, $P = C - (R + FU)$ or $P = A - R$. However, these formulae are not used in practice because the values on the right side of the equations 4.1 and 4.2 are also only estimated. It is advisable to determine the value of P independently and formulae $P = A - R$ and $P = C - (R + FU)$ should be used only for the confirmation of the accuracy of estimation of the components of the population energetic budget.

It might appear simple, on paper, to calculate production by means of the formula, given above, which defines turnover ($P = \bar{B} \cdot \Theta$; formula 1.11). However, this method of calculating production (P) is not practicable owing to the difficulty of determining biomass turnover (Θ) in practice. Although turnover of individuals (Θ_N) can be measured (see 3.1.4 and 3.3), there is still no satisfactory way to convert this into biomass turnover (Θ). Nor can we determine Θ from ecological data: the only method at present available

being to calculate it from production ($\Theta = \dfrac{P}{\bar{B}}$) for which purpose formula

1.11 can be used.

4.2 Population production due to reproduction (P_r) and the number of young born (v_r)

The production due to reproduction is defined by the following formula:

$$P_r = v_r \cdot W_r \quad \ldots\ldots\ldots\ldots\ldots\ldots\ldots\ldots\ldots\ldots\ldots\ldots\ldots\ldots\ldots\ldots\ldots \quad 4\cdot4$$

Determination of the mean value of body weight of newborn (W_r) does not require discussion; in general it is not difficult to find by empirical means. It is enough to weigh a sufficient number of newborn (or eggs) and calculate the mean value of body weight. However, to obtain empirical information about the number of newborn (v_r) over a given time period T is very difficult in field conditions. It is possible only when we can count, within a definite representative area and with sufficient accuracy, the number of young born during the entire reproductive period. This is possible in large vertebrata, or when counting the nests and number of eggs inside the nests in certain birds, or by egg clutches and their size in some insects*. Then we can determine directly $P_r = v_r \cdot W_r$. Most often, however, we have to calculate the number of young born during an arbitrary time period.

To calculate the number of young born (v_r) in a given time period Tv we have to be in possession of at least the following empirical data:

1 L – litter size.

2 t_p – duration of pregnancy: in oviparous animals this demands knowledge of the time from fertilization to hatching and of the standing crop count of pregnant females; in species laying eggs the time period from the laying of the egg to hatching (t_e) is required together with information concerning standing crop count of eggs (nests, and clutch size).

3 N_p – average numbers of pregnant females (standing crop) or numbers

of females and pregnancy ratio $f = \dfrac{N_p}{N_\female}$ or population numbers $\bar{N}$ and preg-

nancy ratio (f) as well as sex ratio $S = \dfrac{N_\female}{N}$.

---

* The single count of eggs (or young born), i.e. of standing crop, is not sufficient for determining v_r because at a given time some eggs may have already been hatched whilst others have not yet been laid.

Various modifications of the two basic methods for determining the number of newborn (v_r) are possible. These methods are based on:
1 Calculating the mean value of the daily birth rate (b), i.e. number of young born per statistical individual per day.
2 Assuming exponential population growth and calculating the instantaneous rate of increase of the population.

4.2.1 Principles for the determination of the number of newborn

4.2.1.1 *By means of average daily birth rate* (b)
This method with certain modifications was indicated (but not used for calculation of v_r) by Edmondson (1960) for rotifers, used for calculations of production in *Copepoda* and *Cladocera* by Winberg, Pečen and Suškina (1965) and for small rodents by Bujalska, Andrzejewski and Petrusewicz (1968). It was analyzed theoretically and the accuracy of the results was estimated in the Institute of Ecology, Polish Academy of Sciences by Petrusewicz (1968).

This method of v_r determination depends on the following reasoning:
If the litter size is L and the pregnancy time is t_p then:

The average number of young born daily by 1 pregnant female $= \dfrac{L}{t_p}$

The average number of young born to one female $= \dfrac{L}{t_p} \cdot f$

Hence daily birth rate of the population (the number bred by an average individual of the population per day):

$$b = \frac{L \cdot f \cdot s}{t_p} \quad \dotfill \quad 4.5$$

the sex ratio s is assumed to be $\frac{1}{2}$, then:

$$b \approx \frac{L \cdot f}{2t_p} \quad \dotfill \quad 4.5a$$

If the average numbers of individuals during time T is $\bar{N}$ then:

$$v_r = \bar{N}_p \cdot T \cdot b = \frac{\bar{N} \cdot T \cdot f \cdot s}{t_p} \cdot L \dots\dots\dots\dots\dots\dots\dots\dots\dots\dots\dots\dots 4.6$$

or assuming $S = \frac{1}{2}$ then:

$$v_r \approx \frac{\bar{N} \cdot T \cdot f}{2t_p} \cdot L \dots\dots\dots\dots\dots\dots\dots\dots\dots\dots\dots\dots 4.6a$$

Because $\bar{N}_p = \bar{N} \cdot f \cdot s$ and so:

$$v_r = \frac{L}{t_p} \bar{N}_p \cdot T \dots\dots\dots\dots\dots\dots\dots\dots\dots\dots\dots\dots 4.6b*$$

The following interesting, and often important, consequences should be noted:

the time interval between litters (clutches) of an average female is: t_p/f

the time period between litters (clutches) of an average individual is: $t_p/(f \cdot s)$

the number of births in time T to $1\female$ pregnant $= T/t_p$

the number of births in time T to 1 female $= T \, f/t_p$

the number of births in time T to 1 individual $= T \, f \, s/t_p$

The following formulae, at first sight very different, can be shown to converge when the symbols are standardised,

Winberg *et al.* (1965):

$$v_r = \frac{\bar{N} \cdot T \cdot s \cdot L}{t_b}$$

* In equations 4.6, 4.6a and 4.6b it is better to calculate value $N \cdot T$ (the number of individual-days), by integrating numerically i.e. calculating the area under the curve drawn from population dynamics data by counting squares or by planimetry for instance. The result will be much more accurate if we have several time points, distributed unequally over the period of investigation (see 3.1.3). Also average mean values of f and s can be obtained by dividing suitable areas:

$$f = N_p \, T/N_\female \, T \text{ and } s = N_\female \, T/N \, T$$

where $t_b = t_p/f$ defines the time between clutches, Edmondson (1960);

$$v_r = \frac{No_e T}{t_b} = \frac{No_e T \cdot f}{t_p} \quad (s = 1 \text{ and } L = 1)$$

Bujalska, Andrzejewski and Petrusewicz (1968):

$$v_r = \frac{\bar{N}_p T \cdot L}{t_p}$$

and Golley (1960):

$$v_r = \frac{N \cdot T \cdot f}{t_p} \ln(\frac{L}{2} + 1)$$

4.2.1.2 *The calculation of the number of newborn on the assumption of exponential population growth*

If the population suffered no losses, its numbers after time T would be N'_T (Edmondson's N calculated—see Fig. 4.1), and the number of individuals born during time T (in the absence of immigration) would be $v_r = N'_T - N_0$ (Fig. 4.1). On the further assumption that the increase of population through reproduction is exponential, we would have, after time T:

$$N'_T = N_0 \cdot e^{\beta T} \dotfill 4.7$$

where β is a constant, the instantaneous birth rate of the population.
   Hence the number of the individuals born in time T would be:

$$v_r = N'_T - N_0 = N_0(e^{\beta T} - 1) \dotfill 4.8$$

N_0 is found empirically; β can be arrived at by the following reasoning: if N_0 represents one pair in which the female is pregnant it will grow after the pregnancy period ($T = t_p$) to $N't_p = L + 2$; introducing this into equation 4·7

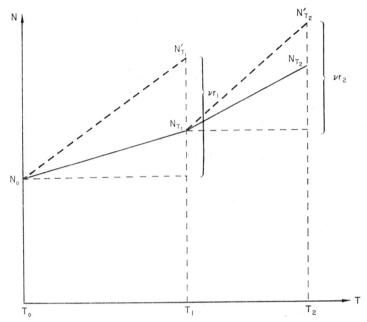

Figure 4.1. Calculation of number of individuals 'produced' (born ν_r) using 'calculated numbers' N'_T (numbers after time T if there were no eliminations).

we obtain: $L+2=2\cdot e^{\beta t}p$. Hence the instantaneous birth rate of a population in which all females are gravid would be:

$$\beta^1 = \frac{(\ln\frac{L}{2}+1)}{t_p}$$

If the proportion of gravid females is f, this means that a statistical average female produces young ones every $t_b = t_p : f$, which will make the instantaneous birth rate of an average individual of the population:

$$\beta = \frac{\ln(\frac{L}{2}+1)}{t_b} = \frac{f\cdot\ln(\frac{L}{2}+1)}{t_p} \quad \dots\dots\dots\dots\dots\dots\dots\dots\dots\dots \textbf{4.9}$$

If the population reproduces parthenogenetically, equation 4·9 will, as given by Edmondson (1960), have the form:

$$\beta = \ln \frac{(L+1)}{t_b} = f \cdot \ln \frac{(L+1)}{t_p}$$

Equation 4·9 ignores mortality, because it assumes that every female— new or old—will go on giving birth. Hence it cannot be used except for very brief time intervals. Consequently a modification accounting for mortality is often accepted, namely:

$$N_T = N_0 \cdot e^{(\beta - \eta) \cdot T} \quad \dots \dots \dots \dots \dots \dots \dots \dots \dots \dots \dots \dots \dots \dots \dots \dots \dots \dots 4.10$$

When $\beta - \eta$ is assumed constant (meaning that the population grows exponentially), we have:

$$v_r = N_0 \cdot (e^{(\beta - \eta)T} - 1) = \frac{\bar{N} \cdot T \cdot f \cdot \ln \left(\dfrac{L}{2} + 1\right)}{t_p} \quad \dots \dots \dots \dots \dots \dots \dots 4.11$$

It was used in this form by Golley (1960) for calculating the production of small rodents.

Remembering that $\bar{N}_p = \bar{N} \cdot s \cdot f$ ($\bar{N} = \bar{N}_p / s \cdot f$ and assuming $s = \frac{1}{2}$), we may write equation 4·11 as follows:

$$v_r = \bar{N}_p T \cdot \frac{2 \ln \left(\dfrac{L}{2} + 1\right)}{t_p} \quad \dots \dots \dots \dots \dots \dots \dots \dots \dots \dots \dots \dots \dots \dots \dots 4.11a$$

4.2.1.3 *Discussion of the principles involved in calculating the number of individuals born into a population*
Quantification of the numerical growth of a population through reproduction is an immensely important question not only in productivity studies but in ecological investigations in general. It is therefore useful to consider the accuracy of the equations used and their theoretical foundations.

Comparisons with the real number of births made in model populations (Petrusewicz, 1968) resembling those of small mammals ($L = 5$, $t_p = 20$ days) lead to the following conclusions.

Conclusion 1. Equation 4·8 ($v_r = N_0 \cdot e^{(\beta T - 1)}$) cannot be used except for very short time T between the censuses. Already with $T > 2 \, t_p$ the results become so distorted as to make the equation unsuitable for the quantification of births in a population.

Conclusion 2. Equations 4·6 ($v_r = \bar{N}_p \cdot T \cdot b$)

$$\text{and } 4 \cdot 11 \quad (v_r = \bar{N}_p \cdot T \, \frac{f \cdot \ln (\frac{L}{2} + 1)}{t_p})$$

produce distinctly different results. For conditions resembling those of small mammals ($L = 5$; $t_p = 20$ days), equation 4·6 gives about twice the result of equation 4·11. In most cases the former equation gives results which are unduly high, and the latter unduly low in comparison with the real number of the animals born, but the first are in most cases considerably closer to reality.

Conclusion 3. The accuracy of both equations examined is not the same for all situations in a population. The results obtained with equation 4·6 overestimate more when the number of females rises than when it falls; in the former situation it always gives exaggerated results, and in the latter often but not always. When the number of pregnant females (N_p) declines the results depend on the relation between the number of pregnant females eliminated v_{pE} and standing crop difference ΔN_p; equation 4·6 overestimates when $v_{pE} > \Delta N_p$, and underestimates when $v_{pE} < \Delta N_p$; this may be the situation in autumn, for instance, when the number of pregnant females declines chiefly due to failure of impregnation and not due to deaths. The results obtained with equation 4·6 are closer to reality when the number of pregnant females declines than when it grows.

Summing up the conclusions 2 and 3: the number of births is not a simple function of the average numbers (abundance) of pregnant females but depends also on their dynamics. Let us illustrate this by an empirical example: we have $N_p = 10$, and after $T_1 = t_p = 20$ days we have $N_p = 20$, and again after $T_2 = t_p' = 20$ days we have $N_p = 10$. The average number of pregnant females

($\bar{N}_p$) will, for both periods, be the same: $\bar{N}_p = 15$ ($\bar{N}_p T = 300$). The number of young born will be, for the first period 50 (assuming no mortality) because none of the ten females that became pregnant during time $T = t_p$ will give birth in that time period; only the ten females which were pregnant at the first census will produce young ones. In the second period the maximum number of animals born will be 100, if all $\bar{N}_p = 20$ managed to give birth before death, and the minimum will be 50, if none of the 10 pregnant females that were lost managed to give birth before death. Finally, assuming that half of the ten females that were lost managed to give birth and the other half did not—an assumption very probable for large numbers and, incidentally, the only one acceptable—there will be 75 animals born in the second period. In the same way the 'reproductive capacity' $\bar{N}_p = (100 + 120) \div 2 = 110$ is not equivalent to $\bar{N}_p = (80 + 140) \div 2 = 110$. In the first case there will be 500 animals born and in the second 400 in time $T = t_p$ (assuming no mortality).

It may thus be said that even when $\bar{N}$ ($\bar{N}_p$), L, and t_p are known accurately, the two equations afford different and variable estimates of the number of animals born, the error being inherent in the equations themselves. The root of this error, which the two equations share, is that the birth rate, a quantity relatively constant and peculiar to a given species, is multiplied by the ecologically variable value of individual-days of pregnant females ($\bar{N}_p T = \bar{N} \cdot s \cdot f \cdot T$); the constant and specific birth rate is in equation 4.6 the daily birth rate per average pregnant female L/t_p, and in equation 4.11 the instantaneous birth rate per pregnant female, i.e.: $2 \ln \left(\dfrac{L}{2} + 1\right)/t_p$. Although the values of

L and t_p vary to some extent within a species, too, they do so within a relatively small range only, being physiologically determined and obligatory. For instance, the average size litter for *Clethrionomys glareolus*—determined from extensive material by Zejda (1966)—varies between 5.4 in spring and 4.6 in autumn. These are average values and, obviously, particular litters may number from one to nine. However, for an adequately large sample the average value may be taken to give a fairly good estimate for a rather wide range of geographical and ecological conditions. The index of reproduction is thus a multiple of the number of individual-days of pregnant females $\bar{N}_p T$ ($= \bar{N} \cdot s \cdot f \cdot T$) which varies with ecological conditions and is thus different for different populations and varies, within populations, rapidly with time. It is a value which must be determined in the area investigated and under actual ecological conditions.

And as has already been shown, the number of animals born depends not only on $\bar{N}_p$ ($\bar{N}_p T$) but also on the dynamics of the numbers of pregnant females.

Conclusion 4. The fourth conclusion that may be drawn from the analysis of methods for determining the number of births is of a more general nature. Namely that it is wrong in principle to assume a geometrical (exponential) population growth in calculating the number of individuals born in a population during a certain time interval. The essence of exponential growth is that what is added (born) reproduces itself at the same rate as what was present previously. Now this is untrue of far the majority of ecological populations, at least over reasonable periods of observation. Pregnant females produce young ones (cause the population numbers to grow). Young ones are born and have to mature and become pregnant before they in turn produce young ones, which means that they begin to share in reproduction much later. So when they are born the numbers of the population do indeed grow, but the fecundity ratio f will fall in the same proportion. Let us consider an extreme case: the number of eggs deposited by a population of cockchafer *Melolontha* sp. in 1968 is not proportional to the growth of the population through reproduction (deposition of eggs and hatching of larvae) in the same year, because it is the females 'born' four years earlier that actually reproduce. Their number is in no way a function of the number of eggs deposited in 1964 but depends on how mild or severe were winters between 1964 and 1968, how abundant were predators in the soil, and so on, and so forth. The same may be said about any species requiring a year or more to mature.

Now let us consider rodents, which are born and begin to reproduce in the same year. Gestation about 20 days + maturation about 35 days + gestation about 20 days make a total of more or less 75 days. If censuses are 40, 60, or 70 days apart not a single one of the animals born in that period will reproduce. Under the conditions occurring, e.g. in Poland, small rodents usually become pregnant in early April. The growth in population numbers in the beginning of July doubles or trebles in comparison with the April level. But the whole growth comes from the previous year's females, the offspring of the current year's females beginning to appear only in July. The population continues to grow, but the numbers of pregnant females usually diminishes, so that there is again no correlation between the population numbers (growth through reproduction) and the numbers of pregnant females. To this it should be added that the equations for reproduction which assume exponential growth of the population are based either on N_0 (equation 4·8) or on $\bar{N}$ (equation 4·6), which means that they do not take into account the dynamics of numbers but merely the average.

Summing up we may say that the number of individuals born in a population is a function of the dynamics of the numbers of pregnant females; the number of pregnant females, on the other hand, is in a very small measure, often practically not at all a function of the number of the individuals born. Calculations of the number of individuals born should not be based on the number of those born during the study period (i.e., on exponential growth) but on the dynamics of numbers of pregnant females.

4.2.1.4 *Calculation of the number of individuals born (v_r) in relation to changes in the numbers and mortality of pregnant females*

Conclusions 3 and 4 tell us that the number of individuals born depends on the dynamics of the numbers of pregnant females. It is therefore right to seek an equation which incorporates direction and magnitude of changes in the numbers of pregnant females.

If there were $\bar{N}_p$ pregnant females within the time equal to the duration of pregnancy ($T = t_p$) then not all of these $\bar{N}_p$ females will deliver young during this period since (1) there are some females which conceived during this time and thus, these females cannot give birth within time-period $T = t_p$ (they will produce litters later), and (2) some of the pregnant females will die before they have brought forth their young. It must be assumed, however, that of those females which were eliminated half will bring forth their young, whereas the other half will not. This assumption is highly probable when large numbers of individuals are dealt with; at least this is the only assumption which can be accommodated.

On this assumption it has been calculated empirically (but it can be also deduced theoretically: Petrusewicz, 1968), that the mean number of pregnant females which will not produce their young during the time $T = t_p$ is:

$$\frac{v_{pE} + \Delta N_p}{2}$$

and the number which will give birth to young is:

$$\bar{N}_p - \frac{v_{pE} + \Delta N_p}{2}$$

where v_{pE} is the number of pregnant females which was eliminated and $\Delta N_p = N_{pT_2} - N_{pT_1}$ is the difference in numbers of pregnant females; this difference (ΔN) should be summed algebraically.

Within the study period T, the duration of pregnancy occurs t_p/T times; thus during time T, the number of new-born individuals will be:

$$(\bar{N}_p - \frac{v_{pE} + \Delta N_p}{2} \cdot \frac{t_p}{T}) \frac{T \cdot L}{t_p}$$

after transforming we obtain:

$$v_r = (\frac{\bar{N}_p \cdot T}{t_p} - \frac{v_{pET} + \Delta N_{pT}}{2}) \cdot L \dots \dots \dots \dots 4.12$$

This formula gives absolutely accurate results (remembering the stated assumption that only half of the eliminated pregnant females will deliver young). Any possible error can result only from inaccuracy in assessing any of parameters $\bar{N}_p$, t_p, v_{pE}, and L.

From the point of view of research practice, equation 4·12 suffers from one defect. It requires knowledge of v_{pE}—the number of pregnant females eliminated—which is a quantity hard to determine under field conditions.

It may be of some help to assume that the mortality rate is the same for pregnant females as for the entire population. Having calculated the general elimination rate we may then calculate the number of eliminated pregnant females with the aid of the equation $N_p = N \cdot s \cdot f$ ($v_{pE} = v \cdot s \cdot f$). However, we very often lack the necessary data for calculating the mortality in a population.

If mortality and consequently v_E cannot be determined we may use during periods of increasing pregnancies, the equation:

$$v_r = (\frac{N_p \cdot T}{t_p} - \frac{\Delta N_p}{2}) L \dots \dots \dots \dots 4.13$$

which at such periods gives a better approximation than equation 4·6. At the time of declining numbers of pregnant females we may use equation 4·6. But it has to be borne in mind that when the mortality is high (and v_{pE} large) in a population, we obtain only rough estimates with the aid of the above mentioned calculation.

4.2.2 Production of newborn

The share of production (P) due to reproduction (P_r) and of production due to body growth (P_g) of individuals present in the population may vary much.

Phillipson (1967a) found that in *Oniscus asellus* the yearly production of one individual under natural conditions amounts to:
$P_r = 8.477$ cal/g live wt/yr and $P_g = 2.718$ cal/g live wt/yr, and thus $P_r = 76\%$ whilst $P_g = 24\%$.

Klekowski, Prus and Żyromska-Rudzka (1967) found that the entire production of a single individual of *Tribolium castaneum* amounts to 66 Kcal/per individual during its life. Production of eggs (P_r) amounts to as much as 60 Kcal/per individual and thus P_r reaches 91% of entire production. It should be remembered, however, that the data of Klekowski *et al.* (1967) refer to the individual. The contribution of P_r per individual, especially when bred in laboratory conditions, is smaller than P_r of a whole population because, in the great majority of cases the length of life of the individual in a free ranging population (ecological longevity) is shorter than physiological length of life; hence not all females in the population attain their reproductive potentialities, and so less young are born to an average (statistical) female.

How should the production due to reproduction (P_r) in mammals be defined? Should this be the biomass of the newborn or should it include growth of tissue produced by young sucklings? These quantities are very different particularly in altricial mammals. It seems to us justifiable to consider P_r as the entire production achieved at the cost of suckling the mother, as was suggested by Petrusewicz (1967), Petrusewicz and Walkowa (1968), because sucklings are obtaining their nutrition from their mother. Costs of maintenance (R) of the mother during the lactation period may greatly exceed even the metabolism of the pregnant female (see chapter 6.2) and amount to 200% of the metabolism under normal conditions.

Walkowa and Petrusewicz (1968) found that in a laboratory population of white mice, the production of young up to 3 weeks of age (they cease sucking at that time) amounts to 46% of the entire production. The production of young up to the 18th day of life (the young start obtaining supplementary food at 15 days) amounts to 43%, whereas production of newborn amounts to 19% of the entire production.

From investigations of a wild but confined (island) population of *Clethrionomys glareolus* it was found that while the live weight of newborn amounts to 16% the production up to three weeks (i.e. approximately P_r) amounts to 57% of the entire production.

We still do not have enough data concerning the participation of P_r and P_g in P, however it may be supposed that in large animals, when the standing crop is stable, body growth (P_g) predominates. However, in small species, with a high turnover (Θ) the lion's share of production (P) is due to reproduction (P_r).

Edmondson (1960) and Hillbricht-Ilkowska (1967) were even justified in considering the entire production of rotifers as:

$$P \approx v_r \cdot \overline{W} \ \dots\dots\dots\dots\dots\dots\dots\dots\dots\dots\dots\dots 4.14$$

where $\overline{W}$ represents mean weight of the individual in the population. This procedure undoubtedly overestimates the production because in reality it should be:

$$P = v_r \cdot \overline{W}^+ \dots\dots\dots\dots\dots\dots\dots\dots\dots\dots\dots 4.15$$

where $\overline{W}^+$ represents mean weight at the moment of death, which is undoubtedly lower than the mean weight of the individual in the population. This procedure is, however, justified for organisms in which weight at the time of birth does not depart significantly from weight of adults (e.g. rotifers, protozoa); when there is no other means for calculating P it can be used for microfauna, because: (1) the greater part of production in microfauna consists of P_r (2) extreme difficulty exists in measuring the individual growth rate in weight and thus (3) in attempting to determine growth, considerable errors are made. So it seems, that formula 4·15 in the absence of better methods may be accepted as a comparatively easy and sufficient basis for estimation of production of the true microfauna. This is not true, however, of most members of the soil 'mesofauna' such as, for example Nematoda, Collembola and certain Acarina, because these grow slowly and much of the production is consumed by predators.

For larger animals P_r must be summed with P_g to obtain the entire production.

4.3 Production of a cohort

In investigations of population production great advantages are to be gained if we can distinguish the cohort, i.e. groups of individuals born in a relatively short time. It allows one to construct the survival and mortality curves from standing crop figures, and to determine without much difficulty the ecological length of life as well as other parameters necessary for the quantification of population production (P). Therefore we will try to analyse in more detail methods of calculating production for populations in which we are able to distinguish separate cohorts.

The ease of calculating production of a cohort depends on whether:

(1) The time interval between day of birth and any census (see Fig. 4.2) is, simply, the absolute age of the individuals in the cohort. In this way we obtain, to some extent automatically, the ecological length of life—one of the most essential parameters and one which is outstandingly difficult to measure in field research.

(2) Successive measurements of numbers (N) allow one to trace the ecological survival curve. The difference in numbers between successive censuses represent individual elimination (loss in time (T_2-T_1) $(N_{(T_1)}-N_{(T_2)})=\Delta N_{(TI)}=v_{E(T_I)}$. Thus it is possible to obtain the mortality curve, and to calculate the survival function (for example an exponential function), or to present it graphically plotting the loss value against the time unit [for example, in days: ΔN: $T_I=(NT_1-NT_2)$: T_I] in the middle of time period $T_I=T_2-T_1$ (Fig. 3.10).

(3) Mean weight (W_{T_1}) of individuals at the moment of census represents mean weight of individuals at the age of the cohort. The increase in mean weight reveals the weight gain for the time period between censuses T_2-T_1. It allows one to trace the individual growth curve and the individual weight gain curve (see Fig. 3.6 and 3.5A).

Being in possession of above mentioned data we can determine the production of a cohort for a given period of time in several ways.

Method 1. We calculate (Fig. 4.2) individual elimination for the time $(T_I=T_2-T_1)$ in question: $v_{E_I}=N_{T_1}-N_{T_2}=\Delta N_{T_I}$ and multiply it by the weight gain up to the first half of the time period in question $(\Delta W_T/_2)$ (assumption: on average, the individuals were eliminated at the intermediate instant of time and so body weight after the first half of T_I represents the weight at the time of death); thus we obtain the production of eliminated

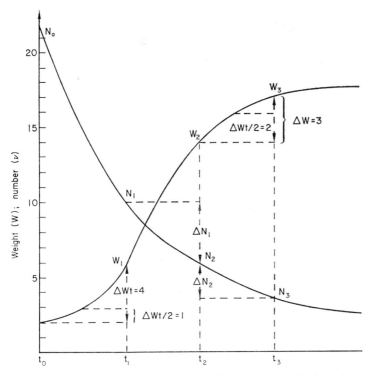

Figure 4.2. Individual growth and survivorship curves as basis for calculation the production.

individuals $(N_1 - N_0)\Delta W_T/_2$. Next we add the product of body weight gain of survivors (ΔW) by the number of surviving individuals (production of survivors). In this way we obtain the entire production due to body growth for the time T_I:

$$P_{g_{T_I}} = \Delta N_{T_I} \cdot \Delta W_T/_2 + N_{T_2} \cdot \Delta W \quad \dots\dots\dots\dots\dots\dots\dots\dots\dots\dots 4.16$$

Note: Body weight gain up to the half time T_I, i.e. $\Delta W_T/2$ does not have to be equal to half of the weight gain for the whole period T_I (Fig. 4.2). Only in cases when body weight gain for the period investigated of time T_I is rectilinear $W_{(T:\,2)} = \dfrac{\Delta W}{2}$ does the formula 4.16 take on the form: $(N_{T_1} - N_{T_2}) \cdot \dfrac{\Delta W}{2}$

$$P_{g_{T_I}} = (N_{T_1} - N_{T_2}) \cdot -\frac{\Delta W}{2} + N_{T_2} \cdot \Delta W \quad \dots\dots\dots\dots\dots\dots\dots \quad 4.17$$

It is easy to verify, that formula 4.17 and 4.19 are identical.

Having calculated the production for several periods of time we now calculate the production sum for successive periods fo time:

$$P_{g_T} = \sum_{i=1}^{i=k} P_{g_i} \dots\dots\dots\dots\dots\dots\dots\dots\dots\dots\dots\dots\dots\dots\dots\dots 4.18$$

where k represents the number of censuses in time T.

Method 2. Assumption: during the time T, on average $\bar{N}_{T_I} = (N_{T_1} + N_{T_2})/2$ individuals exist and produce. Every individual will produce on average $\Delta W_I = W_{T_2} - W_{T_1}$. From the survival and individual growth curves (Fig. 4.2) we get:

$$P_{g_{T_I}} = \frac{N_{T_1} + N_{T_2}}{2} (W_{T_2} - W_{T_1}) = \bar{N}_{T_I} \cdot \Delta W_{T_I} \dots\dots\dots\dots\dots\dots 4.19$$

Next we add already known production figures for individual segments of time:

$$P_{g_T} = \sum_{i=1}^{i=k} \bar{N}_{T_i} \cdot \Delta W_{T_i} \dots\dots\dots\dots\dots\dots\dots\dots\dots\dots\dots\dots\dots\dots 4.20$$

To obtain complete production we should add the weight of newborn or eggs* to the results calculated from formulae 4.16 to 4.20.

---

* There is a risk that frequent weighing of pregnant females will cause inflated estimates of P_g. This error is not very significant because only in advanced pregnancy is weight of foetuses so considerable as to influence the results. For example in mice where duration of pregnancy is 21 days, weight of foetus at 14th day still amounts only to 0·01 mg. Thus the probability of weighing the female in the last days of pregnancy is rather low.

Method 3. Assumption: eliminated individuals increase uniformally in weight in every segment of time. For time segment T_I, production of eliminated specimens may be expressed as follows:

$$E_I = (N_1 - N_2) \cdot \frac{W_1 + W_2}{2} = \Delta N_{T_I} \cdot \overline{W}_{T_I}$$

Thus elimination for k time segments will be:

$$E_T = \sum_{i=1}^{i=k} (\Delta N_{T_i} : \overline{W}_i)$$

Next we must add the production of survivors to the end of the entire time period investigated T, that is $N_T \cdot W_T$:

$$P = \sum_{i=1}^{i=k} (N \cdot \overline{W})_i + N_T \cdot W_T \dots\dots\dots\dots\dots\dots\dots\dots\dots\dots 4.21$$

Method 4. For the cohort, the general number of discrete individuals (v) present in the population represents the initial numbers. With the aid of the survival or mortality curve we can find the mean age of the specimen and read off from the individual growth curve the weight of individuals of mean age (Wī) then:

$$P = v \cdot W\bar{t} \dots\dots\dots\dots\dots\dots\dots\dots\dots\dots\dots\dots 4.22$$

This formula gives only a rough estimation because accurate estimates would demand not the weight at mean age (Wī) but the weight at the moment of death $(\overline{W}^+)$ and thus $P = v : \overline{W}^+$ (cf. formula 4.15). Calculating production of laboratory white mice in this way Walkowa and Petrusewicz (1967) obtained a value P amounting to 184% of the true production value. It was enough, however, to divide the 80 weeks of mouse life time into three parts (not chosen at random but selected from the point of view of the shape of the individual growth curve) to obtain on average 107%, or dividing it into 5 segments of time to obtain 105% of actual production value. Formula 4.22 can be recommended for organisms in which weight at time of birth does not depart much from the weight of very quickly growing adults. Edmondson (1960) and Hillbricht-Ilkowska (1968) estimated production of rotifers, multiplying the number of produced individuals (v_r) by the mean weight of individuals in the population. This can be recommended for quantification of the production of Protozoa and possibly for the smallest soil micro-fauna.

Method 5. Allen (1951) introduced an interesting graphical method for measuring the production of a cohort with the aid of the growth-survivorship curve which has since been used by Ness and Dugdale (1959). This involves plotting the number of individuals in a cohort against the mean individual weight (Fig. 4.3) for the entire history of a cohort, or for a certain, investigated period of time. The area under the growth-survivorship curve represents the production. In this way we can read with ease production for any given time period (substituting individual weight for time).

The growth-survivorship curve allows one to calculate or differentiate the following interesting concepts (Fig. 4.3).

(1) Area $N'_0 N_0(25)O$ production (realized net production of Ness and Dougdale, 1959; Clarke, Edmondson and Ricker, 1946).

(2) Area $N'_0 N_0 N_7(5)$ represents directly the production of eliminated specimens or elimination (E), i.e. production realized but 'given away' to other organisms during time period T.

(3) Area $N'_0 C(25)(O)$ 'potential' production. This concept represents the maximum quantity of material (energy) which could have been elaborated, if there had been no mortality.

(4) Area $N'_0 N_0(1,6)(O)$—production of newborn animals.

(5) The rectangle from any point from the growth-survivorship curve is the biomass at the chosen time moment.

Usually the differences between the results obtained by all five of the above-mentioned methods are not great, only method 4 is markedly different and gives distinctly unsatisfactory results. Therefore this method should be applied solely to estimate the production of very small animals, where growth does not play a significant part (for example Protozoa).

It seems that the most convenient and useful method is that of growth-survivorship curve.

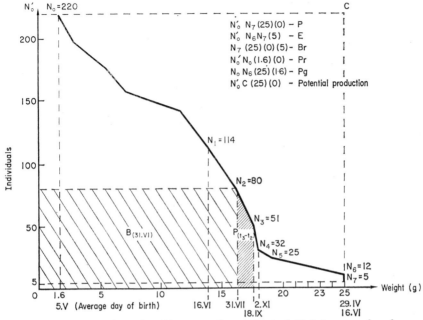

Figure 4.3. Growth-survivorship curve of one cohort of *Clethrionomys glareolus* (data from Petrusewicz *et al.,* 1968).

The number of the cohort plotted against weight, which is entered on the abscissa. The area below survivorship curve represents production; remaining explanations in the text.

In the following circumstances we are able to distinguish a cohort in field investigations.

1. In populations of species reproducing only once during the lifetime, and having a definite, relatively short reproduction period, so that the whole population is of uniform age, with the exception of the short period of time when last year's and the new year's cohort exist side by side and when they are easily distinguished. As an example we can name here investigations on: grasshoppers (Odum and Smalley, 1959; Smalley, 1960) certain spiders (Breymeyer, 1967) winter moth and some other Lepidoptera (Varley, 1967).

2. Populations reproducing several times during a life time but with a definite reproduction period in which we can distinguish overlapping individuals of different cohorts, at least up to the moment of reaching full development. As an example there are arthropods having easily distinguishable develop-

ment stages, in particular Isopoda investigated by Saito (1935); *Onychiurus,* (Healey, 1968) or animals with such long intervals between reproductive periods that in spite of lack of development stages we are able to distinguish overlapping generations (cohorts).

Differentiation of overlapping generations of different year classes may be achieved in certain mammals which reproduce once yearly, in altricial birds in which the whole, or a great deal of the body growth takes place in the nestlings before they are able to fly (Pinowski, 1967—investigations of *Passer montanus*) and so on. Unclassifiable adult individuals can then be treated as one 'cohort' because their weight changes little or not at all after gaining adulthood.

3. In animals, which because of their sedentary way of life are territorially separated into uniform age groups, for example, nymphs of *Philaena* (Homoptera) (Wiegert, 1964) or certain colonies of Acarina.

4. In exceptional cases when isolated populations have been fully marked, for example, investigations of small rodents made by Gliwicz *et al.* (1968).

5. In animals of which we are able to estimate the age of individual animals and thus to estimate the age structure. From changes of age structure in time, it is possible to draw the survivorship curve of the population.

6. Winberg, Pečen and Šuškina (1965) describe an interesting attempt to reduce to a 'cohort' structure a population which has continual reproduction (Copepoda, Cladocera) but also has easily distinguishable stages. This is based on the physiological length of development of separate stages (see 4.5). Such methods are suitable for investigation of invertebrata possessing defined development phases.

However, in a majority of species of vertebrates, populations are such a mixture of generations, that knowledge of age-structure does not allow one to distinguish separate generations and trace their fate in time. In these cases we have to use some other methods of estimating the production.

4.4   Estimation of production based on specific growth rate

4.4.1   Average daily growth gain

Knowing the weight of an individual in a population (single species) at two instants in its life and the time between those two instants (t) we can—as stated previously (3.2.2)—determine the rate of weight gain. The absolute rate will be the weight gain per day* per individual:

$$v = \frac{W_t - W_0}{t} = \frac{\Delta W}{t} \dots\dots\dots\dots\dots\dots\dots\dots\dots\dots\dots\dots \text{[formula 3.9]}$$

Relative specific growth rate consists of weight gain per day per unit of weight:

$$v' = \frac{(W_t - W_0) \cdot 2}{t \cdot (W_t + W_0)} = \frac{\Delta W}{t \cdot \overline{W}} \dots\dots\dots\dots\dots\dots\dots\dots \text{[formula 3.10]}$$

Knowing the time distribution of numbers or biomass of the population for the period of investigation T we can calculate biomass growth (production P) for this period of time:

$$P_g = v \cdot \overline{N} \cdot T \dots\dots\dots\dots\dots\dots\dots\dots\dots\dots\dots\dots\dots\dots\dots 4.23$$
$$P_g = v' \cdot \overline{B} \cdot T \dots\dots\dots\dots\dots\dots\dots\dots\dots\dots\dots\dots\dots\dots\dots 4.24**$$

Of course to take the average daily growth (v and v') for the whole life-time, would result in serious errors because growth rate varies depending on the age of individual (see Fig. 3.6). Therefore, v_s and v'_s should be determined for individual development stages if there are any, or for various age classes —if we have the means to determine the age of animals—or at least for various weight classes assuming that the weight corresponds with the age of the animals, and that animals of uniform weight have the same average daily growth gain. Knowing the numbers of corresponding phases of development stages, age or weight classes, we can find the production of those stages (P_{g_s}) for investigated period of time T:

$$P_{g_s} = v_s \cdot \overline{N}_s \cdot T \dots\dots\dots\dots\dots\dots\dots\dots\dots\dots\dots\dots\dots\dots 4.25$$
$$P_{g_s} = v'_s \cdot \overline{B}_s \cdot T \dots\dots\dots\dots\dots\dots\dots\dots\dots\dots\dots\dots\dots\dots 4.26$$

where s represents a given stage of development.

* For large animals weekly or monthly weight gain can be measured.

** Concerning the determination of individual-day $N \cdot T$ value and $\overline{B} \cdot T$ quantity of biomass-days see 3.1.3.

Then the entire production due to body growth P_g for time period T is:

$$P_g = \sum_{s=1}^{s=m} v_s \cdot N_s \cdot T \quad\dots\dots\dots\dots\dots\dots\dots\dots\dots\dots\dots\dots\dots \text{4.27}$$

$$P_g = \sum_{s=1}^{s=m} v'_s \cdot \bar{B}_s \cdot T \quad\dots\dots\dots\dots\dots\dots\dots\dots\dots\dots\dots\dots \text{4.28}$$

To estimate the entire production we should, according to formula 4.3 $(P = P_g + P_r)$ add the value P_r. However, it should be remembered that $\bar{B} \cdot T$ may contain partly the weight of foetuses in pregnant females.

Production estimation by means of formulae 4.27 and 4.28 seems to apply to all ecological and systematic types of animals, excluding possibly microfauna where it is better to estimate the production using P_r (see 4.2.2) because in those small animals determination of average daily growth gain appears to be difficult and also liable to great errors.

Estimation of production by means of daily average growth gain allows us to avoid troublesome determinations of the length of life (t), determination of the discrete number of individuals present (v), or mortality (η) and birth rate. Accuracy of daily average growth gain determination depends on ability to distinguish as many developmental stages (age or weight classes) as possible, and establishment of their quantity ($\bar{B}_s \cdot T$ or $\bar{N}_s \cdot T$).

4.4.2 Instantaneous growth rate

Assuming exponential growth of an average individual we can—as stated previously (3.2.2)—find instantaneous rate of weight gain as follows:

$$q = \frac{\ln W_{t_2} - \ln W_{t_1}}{t_2 - t_1} \quad\dots\dots\dots\dots\dots\dots\dots\dots\dots\dots\dots \text{[formula 3.1.2]}$$

where W_{t_2} and W_{t_1} are the weight at instants t_2 and t_1 of an individual's life. Now, assuming that growth of population biomass is constant (population growth curve is exponential) we can calculate B'_T, i.e. B calculated at any interval of population biomass, if there is no mortality:

$$B'_T = B_0 \cdot e^{qT} \quad\ldots\ldots\ldots\ldots\ldots\ldots\ldots\ldots\ldots\ldots\ldots\ldots\ldots\ldots\ldots 4.29$$

and the production for time period T:

$$P = B'_T - B_0 = B_0(e^{q \cdot T} - 1) \quad\ldots\ldots\ldots\ldots\ldots\ldots\ldots\ldots\ldots\ldots 4.30$$

Formula 4.30 can be used only for a very short time; for $T > 2t_p$ the results are unrealistic.

Modifications of the formula 4.30 are widely known amongst ecologists thanks to works of Ricker (1946). He tried to determine, how much biomass of the population there would be after time T if the growth due to simultaneously occurring individual growth and mortality was exponential:

$$B_T = B_0 \cdot e^{(q-\eta) \cdot T} \quad\ldots\ldots\ldots\ldots\ldots\ldots\ldots\ldots\ldots\ldots\ldots\ldots\ldots 4.31$$

where q—represents specific instantaneous growth rate of the population (formula 3.12) and η—mortality rate. Knowing birth rate (β) mortality rate can be found, having two reliable standing crop counts for the cohort, using formula $N_T = N_0 \cdot e^{(\beta-\eta) \cdot T}$ and

$$\beta - \eta = \frac{\ln N_T - \ln N_0}{T} \quad\ldots\ldots\ldots\ldots\ldots\ldots\ldots\ldots\ldots\ldots 4.32$$

where N_T and N_0 represent standing crop counts for the cohort separated by an optional period T; birth rate (β) can be determined using formula 4.9. Hence production for time T will equal the result of the subtraction: calculated biomass (B'_T) less initial biomass (B_0) after the analogy of calculated and initial biomass regardless of mortality used in the formula (4.30 and 4.31):

$$P_T = B'_T - B_0 = B_0(e^{(q-\eta)T} - 1) \quad\ldots\ldots\ldots\ldots\ldots\ldots\ldots\ldots 4.33$$

for simplification this is often expressed as follows: $P_T = B_0 [\exp(q - \eta) - 1]$.

The formula 4.33 is attractive for the ease with which field information may be obtained—only one standing crop count is necessary—but is, however, subject to reservations:

(1) the formula is based on the assumption that $(q - \eta)$ is constant, which is true only for short periods of time.

(2) determination of the values q and η requires much mathematical calculation. A relatively small error in determination of N_T and N_0 values (formula 4.32) may result in large errors in calculation of η. Also when determining q (formula 3.12) the error in values of W_1 and W_0 will result in errors in the value of q. Finally, when we raise to a power $(e^{(q-\eta)T})$ the result may well depart widely from reality.

4.5 Estimations of production based on specific longevity

Production of animals with distinguishable developmental stages may be estimated when the physiological time of development (t_s) and numbers $(\bar{N}_s)$ of a given phase are known (Winberg, Pečen and Šuškina, 1965; Kaczmarek, 1967). The number of individuals (v_s) of one phase, which passed into the next during time T is represented by:

$$v_s = \bar{N}_s \frac{T}{t_s} \dots\dots\dots\dots\dots\dots\dots\dots\dots\dots\dots \text{[see formula 3.7]}$$

Winberg *et al.* (1965) considers the number of individuals which passed from the stage under consideration to the next as production (in number of individuals) of the considered stage. When multiplied by weight gain of the same stage one can obtain a production of this phase:

$$P_s = v_s \cdot (W_s - W_{s-1}) = \frac{\bar{N}_s \cdot T}{t_s} (W_s - W_{s-1}) \dots\dots\dots\dots\dots\dots 4.34$$

Consequently, adding the production of several phases, Winberg *et al.* (1965) distinguished four stages: eggs $(t_e, \bar{N}_e)$, nauplius $(t_I, \bar{N}_I)$, copepodite (t_{II}, N_{II}) and adult $(\bar{N}_m)$, he obtains production of entire population (all phases) for the time T:

$$P = \left[\frac{N_m \cdot s \cdot L}{t_b} \cdot We + \frac{N_e}{t_e} (W_I - W_e) + \frac{N_I}{t_I} \cdot (W_{II} - W_{IJ}) + \frac{N_{II}}{t_{II}} (W_m - W_{II}) \right] \cdot T$$

$$\dots\dots 4.35$$

where t_b represents the time between broods ($t_b = t_p \div f$ see 4.2). The first expression of this sum represents the production of adults due to reproduction (P_r) on the assumption of no weight gain in adults. Accepting that the initial value of I phase (nauplius, W_I) equals weight of egg (W_e), the second expression of the sum equals zero, which simplifies the sum to three components. In investigations of insects with non-feeding phases (egg, pupae) we may accept the production of these phases as zero (lack of consumption, and so the lack of accumulation of their own tissue).

The calculations of Winberg *et al.* (1965) were based on 3 to 10 field censuses each month, from which the average density of each stage ($\bar{N}_s$) was calculated. In addition the physiological time of development and the weight of each phase were obtained in the laboratory. A correction was made for variation of specific longevity (t_s) in relation to temperature.

Winberg *et al.* (1965) indicate still another interesting graphical way of calculating production with the aid of specific development time (t_s), weight of individuals in a given phase (W_s) and mean numbers N_s. Monthly mean numbers of individuals (N_s) is divided by development time of this phase expressed in days, getting in this way mean daily number of individuals which pass to the next stage ($v_s = \dfrac{\bar{N}}{t_s} \cdot T$ at $T = 1$; see 3.1.4). This daily mean was centered on the median interval of the phase development time, giving a survival curve of individual phases (Fig. 4.4C). Next having obtained from laboratory investigations, an individual growth curve (Fig. 4.4A) he divides the phase increment by the time of duration of this phase (longevity), and thus obtains the daily growth gain of a given phase. Then the latter value is related to the intermediate moment of the phase (Fig. 4.4B). Thus we arrive at a daily weight gain curve. Next we trace the products of: the number of survivors (from the curve C) times daily weight gain (from the curve B) giving a diagram the surface of which represents daily production of all phases (of population). Multiplying by 30 we obtain monthly body growth (P_g). If we add to it production due to reproduction (P_r) we obtain P. It seems that the principles of calculation just mentioned hold great promise. Especially attractive is the fact that rather few field data are needed. It is essential, however, to distinguish developmental phases accurately to determine the mean numbers in each. The development time and weight of individual phases may be established under laboratory conditions.

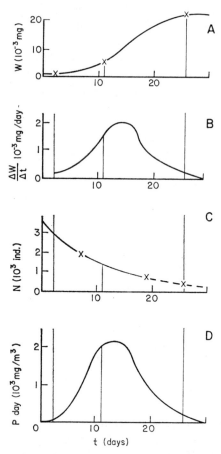

Figure 4.4. Calculation of production using the graphical method, Winberg (1965, 1968).

Abscissa: development time of egg (t_e), nauplius (t_{s1}), copepodite (t_{s2}), in days. A, individual growth curve in 10^{-3} mg fresh wt (empirical data); B, curve of absolute growth gain ($\Delta W / _{\Delta t}$) in 10^{-3} mg day (calculated from curve A); C, survivorship curve of subsequent stages calculated by dividing the average monthly abundance (based on 3–10 censuses) by the duration of development of a given stage (t_s), as placed in the middle of development time for a given stage; D, daily production of subsequent stages, obtained from curve B and C.

5

The Study of Food and Feeding in Relation to Ecology

5.0 The objectives and principles of ecological feeding studies

Although not a component of secondary production in the strict sense, knowledge of food consumption is necessary for productivity studies for two reasons:

1. Assimilation can be calculated either from

$$A = P + R \dotfill 5.1$$

or from

$$A = C - (F + U) \dotfill 5.2$$

It follows that the measurement of assimilation from consumption minus rejection provides an independent check on production plus respiration. In practice this possibility is usually of only theoretical interest because direct measurement of production is more accurate. In the case of some invertebrate populations, however, it is virtually impossible to measure production under conditions which realistically approach those in the field. In this case the indirect approach can be most useful (Engelmann, 1966; Healey, 1967).

2. Any natural population constitutes a place of division in the flow of energy through an ecosystem: on the one hand assimilated material is oxidized or else it is channelled into the living material of the organisms and thus becomes food for predators, parasites and decomposers of flesh. On the other hand un-assimilated material passes (as rejecta) to faeces and excreta and provides the raw materials for quite different food chains. Thus, of the energy in grass eaten by bullocks in a well stocked temperate grassland some 60% is rejected as faeces and only about 4% becomes available to man as meat (Macfadyen, 1964): Beef animals which are kept indoors and fed concentrated food may convert twice as great a proportion of their intake into beef,

a correspondingly smaller amount being used in respiration (Duckham, 1963). In a field study of the small mammals of a beech forest, Grodzinski *et al.* (1968) found that 83% of the total annual food consumption was used for production plus respiration, 13% being lost as faeces and 4% as excreta. Of the assimilated energy 97·7% was respired so that tissue production accounted for only 2·3% of assimilation or 1·9% of consumption. Invertebrate herbivore production ranges from between about 4% and 16% according to Wiegert (1964, 1965) but usually production by primary consumers is less than 10%.

The ratio between these two quantities — assimilated and rejected food— is thus an important index of the effect of a population on subsequent food chains in the community.

In order to convert the different components of feeding equations into a common "currency" it is necessary to determine their calorific values by combustion. Formerly wet combustion methods, using acids, were employed (Ivlev, 1934) but the availability of accurate and relatively simple bomb calorimeters has resulted in their widespread use today. In section 3.2.4 these methods and a range of calorific values were presented.

Two factors largely determine the assimilation/consumption efficiency of a field population. Firstly the nature of the food and the extent to which it is selected by the consumer; these may well vary seasonally, from place to place and during the lifetime of the animal. These topics are presented in sections 5.4.1 to 5.4.3. Secondly digestive efficiency varies with characteristics of the digestive system of the organism. Whilst detailed physiological studies of digestive efficiency are outside the scope of this handbook, a brief consideration of this topic appears in sections 5.4.4 and 5.4.5.

The main purpose of feeding studies in ecology is to estimate the quantitative feeding characteristics of whole populations as they occur under natural conditions. Such direct measurements have never yet been made in the field and in order to arrive at the best possible estimates the ecologist is forced to combine field data on population numbers and composition with laboratory feeding work. Ideally the latter should be made on whole populations in order to account for intra-specific interactions, but once again further compromise is frequently necessary and data from physiological studies of individual animals may be substituted.

All the quantities: consumption, assimilation and rejection as well as others such as production and respiration can be expressed either on a *per capita* basis or in relative terms (i.e. per unit of biomass or even of calorific content of the standing crop (Slobodkin, 1960). The choice as to which basis should be used is once again a matter of the level of generalization which is being attempted. A detailed budget of a single species demands analysis of the effect of age, sex, season and many other factors on these components of the feeding balance sheet and data are best expressed in *per capita* terms.

A wide-ranging study involving many species and with, perhaps, comparisons between trophic levels, cannot normally take full account of the detailed causes of such variability. Since there are frequently large scale differences between the properties of such groups and since it is invalid to compare organisms of very different sizes or feeding habits, a relative basis is then much more suitable and permits simpler calculations.

When relative quantities are used certain well-established effects of body size can usually be assumed — or at least used in a preliminary hypothesis. Most metabolic parameters vary with weight in accordance with a formula of the form (see Kleiber, 1961):

$$y = W^a \dots\dots 5.3$$

in which y = metabolic parameter
W = weight
a = a power of the order of 0·75.

As far as is known this relationship applies to food balance quantities as well as to other metabolic characteristics.

5.1 Consumption of food: qualitative aspects and food selection

Of the food potentially available to an animal, only a small proportion is usually consumed. Highly selective consumers tend to achieve a high assimilation/consumption ratio because their food usually contains more nourishment and because they are better adapted to digest it. Non-selective feeders such as many detritus-consumers have much lower assimilation efficiency (Balogh, 1958b). One of the most difficult factors to quantify in feeding biology is the actual food consumption under field conditions. It has been widely found that food preferences vary considerably according to habitat, time of year, age and even individual characteristics of the animal concerned. The palatability and nutritive value of the food are equally variable. This has been reviewed in the case of large mammals by Milner (1967), whilst

Drożdż (1967, 1968) reports a very complete study of the effect of variation in natural foods on uptake and assimilation efficiency of small mammals. He found the digestibility of pure foods varied from 70% to 90%, that of concentrated diets (nuts and oats) from 84% to 94% whilst herbs were only 74% digestible. The faeces/consumption ratio varied from 7% to 23%. There were also specific differences between the species as follows:

Microtus arvalis   78%
Clethrionomys glareolus   83%
Apodemus flavicollis   86%
Apodemus agrarius   89%

The following is a list of approaches which have been used in investigating the selection process by consumers together with criticisms which may be made in each case.

5.1.1 Direct observation, feeding

The taxonomic identity of plants eaten by hares has been observed with an astronomical telescope by Anderson (1950) and that of sheep by Hunter (1958). Some predators are particularly suitable for studies of this kind including spiders which leave corpses on their webs (Kajak, 1967). The direct observation of prey fed to nestling birds by automatic photographic recording has been particularly successful (Buckner, 1967). However, accurate identification in all these methods is difficult and often impossible.

In certain bird studies, however, accurate identification has been rendered possible by intercepting the food in one way or another. For instance Malčevskij and Kadočnikov (1953), Kluijver (1933) and others have used a ring round the birds' neck to prevent swallowing and thus permit identification of the food. Gibb and Betts (1963) Bouckner (1960) and Czarnecki and Foksowicz (1954) have placed obstructions in the way of the nest and thus have been able to observe the birds' prey from a very closely placed hide. Betts (1956) in a study of Coal Tits made use of an artificial nestling mouth and was able to recover prey deposited there by the parent bird.

A less direct method, particularly suitable for numerous microscopic predators is to compare the populations of food organisms in a microcosm to which predators have been introduced with those in a control microcosm from which they have been excluded. This approach has been used, for instance, by Gliwicz (1969) in studies on the feeding of rotifers. Precautions to allow for growth of the food organisms and to ensure adequate replication must, of course, be taken.

5.1.2 Identification of cuticular plant remains in faeces

This has been carried out on sheep by Martin (1964), who detected a regular yearly sequence of preferences in the species chosen. It has also been done for woodlice (terrestrial isopoda) by Huxley (pers. comm.) and in studies of the food of microarthropods (e.g. Healey, 1965). Similar methods have been widely used in the analysis of remains in the pellets rejected by carnivorous birds (e.g. Southern, 1954). More recent work suggests the possibility of further improvements in the classification and identification of plant remains. In particular Stewart (1967) describes an improved technique for analysing plant epidermis in large herbivore faeces whilst the development of the scanning electron microscope, Oatley (1966), provides an extremely rapid method of examining surface features at resolutions 100 times as great as those visible with the light microscope and has already revealed structural detail of taxonomic value. However, only materials which have survived the processes of digestion remain in the faeces and other rejecta and many of the more digestible foods do not leave traces. This objection applies particularly to carnivores which feed on the more liquid parts of their prey, such as spiders.

5.1.3 Gut contents analysis: dead and living animals

The identification of the contents of the alimentary canal has been widely used for the study of choice of foods and many of the methods mentioned in the above paragraph can be applied here also. The gut contents have been examined from slaughtered wild animals (Adams *et al.*, 1962) and crop analyses have been made from birds (references in Buckner, 1967). Food selection in living sheep, cattle and deer has been studied with the aid of a fistula in the oesophagus or the rumen in order to sample the food selected (references in Milner, 1967). This method has been applied to tame and domestic animals but for obvious reasons it has not yet been adapted for use with wild mammals. Further, the slaughter of animals demanded for accurate statistical analysis of gut contents may involve a large proportion of the population being studied.

5.1.4 Laboratory studies of food preference

Many workers have applied such methods to a wide range of organisms.

Miller (1954) compared the food preferences in the laboratory of two species of small mammals. Healey (1965) presented named species of soil fungi to soil collembola and detected strong preferences for certain species, whilst Wallwork (1958) studied a wide variety of possible food choices presented to oribatid mites. In this type of experiment, however, it may be impossible to provide a realistic range of foods for choice by the animal; also laboratory conditions and the way in which foods are presented may well affect the choice exhibited. In a number of cases laboratory feeding trials have geen supported by field data. For instance Miller, in the above study, compared stomach contents of field animals with his laboratory findings and obtained considerable confirmation of the laboratory results. Coleman and Macfadyen (1966) dug up soil samples, sterilized them with gamma rays, inoculated them with known fungi and replaced them in the soil. They found that the samples tended to be invaded by species of mites and collembola which had been shown by laboratory trials to select those particular fungal species in the laboratory. Clearly in such instances the investigator's confidence in laboratory choice trials is substantially supported by field confirmation.

5.2 The quantitative measurement of consumption

The quantitative measurement of food consumption by confined animals in the laboratory is relatively simple. But to make the same measurements on animals which are free in their natural habitat is usually very difficult. The qualitative methods already discussed in chapter 5.1 (direct observation, the use of fistulas, etc.) have only limited application here. In order to permit extrapolation from laboratory measurements to field data attempts have been made to measure the same quantities under laboratory and field conditions and thus to obtain numerical factors by which to convert from the one situation to the other. However difficult this may be in particular instances, it does offer the possibility of interpreting laboratory measurements. The calculation of such factors requires, of course, to be related to representative life stages, seasons and population conditions. For instance mice under crowded conditions have been shown to consume 13 % more food than when kept at one quarter of the density. In studies on the effects of crowding on social structure of house mouse populations Southwick (1955) noted a fall from 4·20 to 2·40 g of grain consumption per day and in similar work on white mice Petrusewicz (1963) found that consumption of oats fell from 4·0 to 2·8 g per day as population density rose to a peak.

5.2.1 Laboratory type methods

These simply involve the measurement of food uptake from an unlimited supply by periodical weighing in order to determine the difference between food supplied and that remaining after exposure in the feeding trial. Alternatively the increase in weight of the feeding animal may sometimes be determined directly by means of a balance. Such methods are widely used in animal husbandry work (e.g. Brody, 1954). There are frequently practical problems associated with scattering and waste of uneaten food. In the case of smaller animals it is often exceedingly difficult to estimate food uptake even in the laboratory. On the other hand, ingestion by species which consume discrete parts of a plant, especially the fruits of other storage organs, can frequently be measured by counting the numbers actually removed.

5.2.2 Field-based estimations

5.2.2.1 Methods based on measurements of faeces production

A possible (but tedious) method for determining food consumption is to measure faeces production of the animal at liberty and then to derive a relationship between consumption and faeces production in the laboratory. This factor is then applied to the field data in order to calculate the consumption. The method can be refined by allowing for the relative digestibility of different types of food and using the following formula due to Milner (1967) (in which all quantities are measured in terms of dry matter):

$$C = \frac{F}{F/C} \quad \dots\dots\dots\dots\dots\dots\dots\dots\dots\dots\dots\dots\dots\dots\dots\dots\dots\dots\dots\dots\dots\dots\dots\dots\dots 5.4$$

in which C = consumption and F = egestion, F/C being the ratio of faeces to consumption. This method has only been used on captive deer (not on truly wild populations of mammals) but a comparable idea has been applied by Engelmann (1961) to soil mite populations and is evidently of considerably potential value in the case of relatively static organisms whose faeces (and other rejecta) remain in one place for a period of time.

A further and more widely used method of estimating consumption from faeces production is possible when the animal's food contains an indigestible indicator substance. Since substances such as silica are not digested at all, the quantity emerging in faeces will equal that consumed. From the proportion occurring initially in the food, the total food consumption may be readily obtained. This method has been used by Nielsen working with the millipede *Glomeris marginata*, living in a field of *Brachypodium pinnatum* (see Bocock, 1963). It has also been used in studies on vertebrates (see Golley, 1967) who reports that in certain cases the use of partially digestible indicators such as cellulose is also possible (see Short and Remmenga, 1965). The amount of food killed but not used (NU) can sometimes provide a useful quantitative index of food consumption. One example is provided by the study of the feeding of web spinning spiders (Andrzejewska *et al.*, 1967). In this case the corpses of prey after they had been sucked dry, were left in the web and could be counted by the authors. A slightly different problem which has also been solved by the use of tracers, this time in the form of insoluble chemicals, is to determine faeces production in captive animals. By feeding known doses of chromic oxide in the animal's food and by measuring the concentration in representative samples of faeces, the total quantity of faeces produced may be measured (see Milner, 1967).

5.2.2.2   *Population consumption, estimated from laboratory measurements of assimilation and faeces production*

Owing to the practical difficulties involved in the direct measurement of consumption, most authors in practice have found that it is most easily measured as the sum of faeces production and assimilation. The latter, in turn, is calculated from the sum of production and respiration. Since both production and respiration vary with age it is necessary to obtain measurements for a representative range of age classes and other demographically distinct groups (sexes, animals laying down food reserves or producing gametes, etc.). Methods for measuring these component processes are discussed under the relevant sections (Production: parts 3 and 4; faeces production: section 5.2.2.1; respiration, part 6). A valuable pioneer study of this kind is Wiegert's paper on grasshopper populations (Wiegert, 1965).

5.3   Interactions between food stocks and the organisms feeding on them

The direct estimation of consumption under field conditions by comparing the quantities of potential food supplies exposed to, and protected from consumption is rarely a practical proposition. In the case of a grazing herbivore and its plant foods, for instance, plant competition is usually so severe that selective removal of one species is usually followed by a complete change in the balance of competition between remaining species. This, in turn, may modify the herbivore's behaviour, or it may remain strictly selective as, for instance, in Andrzejewska's (1967) study of the homopteran *Cicadella viridis* which refused to eat dicotyledonous plants even when greatly overcrowded. Since it has been shown that earlier stages in a plant succession may have higher primary production than later ones (Odum, 1960) it is clearly unjustifiable to relate changes in primary production to grazing factors only. Conversely, many herbivores damage plants they feed upon to a much greater extent than can be attributed simply to the amount of food consumed. Andrzejewska *et al.* (1967) showed that grasshoppers damage five times as much grass as they actually eat—(i.e. $NU = 5 \times C$), whilst Varley (1967) calculated that defoliating *Lepidoptera* may decrease the primary production of oak trees ten times as much as the loss due to the actual consumption by the caterpillars; however this figure has since been revised by McGregor (1968) to about four times. Similar and very complicated effects have been reported by Dixon (1966) in the case of tree-living aphids. Only in cases where a single food source is being consumed can the consumption by the consumer be determined by difference from exposed and protected sources. One example of a successful direct estimate of consumption is the measurement of the area of tree leaves consumed by herbivorous animals, as has been done by Bray (1961). Since the holes also 'grow' after they have been made by the animal, control holes, punched from the leaves by the observer, must be made to correct for this factor. Leaf areas were measured by means of a graph paper planimeter and the use of the leaf was calculated as a percentage of the missing (i.e. consumed) area. These percentages varied from 3·2 to 15·0 over a range of tree species, the mean value being 8·3 per cent. When related to total primary productivity the minimum estimates of primary consumption obtained in this way amounted to between 0·5 per cent and 1·4 per cent of the total plant production.

An alternative approach is that described by Paris and Sikora (1967) who used isotope-labelled food to determine consumption by the isopod *Armadillidium vulgare*. Leaf discs of known specific activity were fed and the proportion consumed was obtained from the reduction in the activity of the leaf discs which remained after feeding. This approach is clearly only of quantitative significance when the population is a controlled and circumscribed one.

5.4   Digestive efficiency and ratio of assimilation
to consumption

5.4.1   Principles and examples

The energy content of the material actually absorbed through the gut of an animal is always less than that of the food which it consumes.

It will be remembered (section 2.2.1) that assimilation was defined as consumption less rejecta $(A = C - (F + U))$: in other words this allows for the ecologist's practical difficulties in separating from the true faeces the components of nitrogenous and other excretion, as well as metabolised products such as digestive enzymes, mucus and gut lining. On the other hand 'digested energy' was defined as consumption less faeces $(D = C - F)$: in other words it is equal to assimilation plus nitrogenous and other excreta.

Digestive efficiency might, theoretically be defined either in terms of the proportion of consumption which contributes to digestive energy or of that which goes into assimilation, as defined above. In order to avoid confusion and to be consistent with physiological practice, we therefore define 'digestive efficiency' as the ratio of digested energy to consumption:

$$\frac{D}{C} = \frac{C - F}{C} = \frac{C + U - (F + U)}{C} = \frac{A + U}{C} \quad \dots\dots\dots\dots\dots 5.5$$

whilst we refer to the first-named ratio, that of assimilation to consumption as the 'assimilation/consumption efficiency':

$$\frac{A}{C} = \frac{C - (F + U)}{C} \quad \dots\dots\dots\dots\dots\dots\dots 5.6$$

or, when the context renders it quite unambiguous, as 'assimilation efficiency' for short. In practice it is usually only the latter which can be determined and the two ratios will differ by only a few per cent.

Both 'digestive efficiency' and 'assimilation efficiency' are very variable, not only between species (depending on ecological and taxonomic status of the species concerned) but also within the same species (depending on environmental factors, the type and condition of the food, the amount of available food and the physiological condition of the animal at the time). They are also subject to systematic changes throughout the animal's lifetime.

The ecologist who is interested in energy flow between species and through whole systems, must study assimilation/consumption efficiency and attempt to generalise about it. This is because a major split in the flow of energy through the ecosystem occurs at this point: mainly with the allocation of food materials on the one hand to respiration, production of flesh and reproductive products (which will pass eventually to predators and decomposers) and on the other hand, to faeces and urine (which are consumed by coprophagous animals and microbes).

The variability of assimilation efficiency is the main reason why calculations of production, when based on assimilation less respiration, are unreliable in comparison with direct measurements of weight gain. It follows that, in energy budget work on individual organisms, a full analysis of the variability of digestive efficiency is essential. It is only by extending experiments over long periods and many individuals that reliable data can be obtained. The treatment adopted in this section is therefore, firstly to list the major causes of variability and then to illustrate some precise examples of particular instances.

Examples are given firstly of the effect on assimilation efficiency of environmental factors, of characteristics of the food and of internal physiological factors in that order. Consideration is then given to some specific examples of attempts to assess assimilation efficiency from the rates, firstly of faeces plus urine production and secondly of food consumption. Finally the evidence is drawn together on the influence, on assimilation efficiency, of feeding level, nutrient, content of food and other factors.

5.4.2 The effect of environmental factors on assimilation level and efficiency

In general there is, with respect to all physical factors, a range beyond which normal physiological processes break down. In homoitherms this range is usually considerably extended because the animals actively compensate for external change by maintenance of a constant internal environment. But this compensation itself entails metabolic costs and the overall effect of external change on physiology is complex. In most poikilotherms there are temperature levels beyond which no feeding occurs. Within that range various kinds of acclimatisation can occur, for instance in many species of spiders completion of the life cycle demands more than one season in colder climates as compared with a single season in warmer climates (Bristowe, 1933; Edgar,

1968) and extra seasons are needed for full development in many diplopods (Blower, 1968). Presumably such extended life cycles reflect lower rates of production and hence of assimilation, although there will inevitably be a higher total assimilation for the whole life cycle. There is, however, some tendency for acclimatisation in marine benthos organisms (Thorson, 1950). The effect of high and low temperatures on mammals are discussed by Kleiber (1961).

It must always be remembered, however, that static recording of micro-climatic factors may be of little relevance to the conditions actually en-countered by animals and the corresponding metabolic acitivity on account of behavioural features which permit animals to avoid, particularly, more extreme conditions (Macfadyen, 1968).

Although few specific examples are known to the authors, it is probable that assimilation efficiency is very dependent on environmental factors even within the range normally encountered. Thus Cox (1961) found that not only temperature, but also length of daylight is an important determinant of efficiency in tropical Finches. An increase from twelve hours to fifteen hours of daylight led to increased metabolism and more efficient use of food.

5.4.3 The influence of food characteristics on digestive efficiency

The food content and chemical composition of most higher plants varies with season and age of the plant and also with the environmental conditions, especially temperature, sunlight and humidity. These factors alone alter the palatibility and digestibility of plant food, which are difficult to avoid in food consumption studies. As one extreme, for instance, the larvae of *Vanessa urticae* almost refuse to feed if provided with plucked leaves of the nettle *Urtica dioica* and assimilation efficiency falls to a very low level when the leaves loose their turgor in the absence of water. On the other hand the enclosure of foliage, still attached to a plant, within netting sleeves alters the microclimate as well as the transpiration rate and other physiological properties of the plant. This in turn modifies the assimilation efficiency of feeding animals in ways which have not yet been fully analysed.

Apart from such sources of variation within the same plant/herbivore system, even greater differences occur between the properties of different food plants when they are consumed by a more general herbivore. Thus Soo Hoo and Fraenkel (1966a, b) working with polyphagous armyworms *Prodenia eridania* tested the feeding efficiency on eighteen different plants from thirteen families. Ten of these were assimilated efficiently and efficiency values varied from 36 to 76 per cent. Even within the same plant this efficiency was influenced by water content, protein content and fibre content.

The nitrogen content of insect food would appear to have a particularly great effect on overall metabolism; Ito and Fraenkel (1966), for instance, reported a dramatic change in metabolism and increased respiration rate in *Tenebrio molitor* when fed on diets deficient in nitrogen, whilst Mittler (1967) found that the lack of a single amino-acid (Methionine) in the food of *Myzus persicae* halved its food intake.

Soo Hoo and Fraenkel also found that, with one preferred food plant, there was an inverse relationship between assimilation efficiency and the total amount consumed.

The latter feature is a very widespread phenomenon amongst invertebrates; Cushing (1958) found that at times of phytoplankton abundance the Copepod *Temora longicornis* will eat up to five or ten times as much food as it assimilates, whilst at lower food densities more normal efficiencies are usual. Gajevskaya (1959) reports a similar situation among bottom living invertebrates in the Black Sea. A particularly interesting example of the interplay of food characteristics and feeding is given by Gliwicz (1969) in a study of rotifer feeding. These animals select their food purely on the basis of size (and not on nutritive value or chemical composition). In more eutrophic waters the algae tend to be larger and there are greater numbers of bacteria whilst under oligotrophic conditions the algae are smaller and bacteria less numerous. Since the maximum food size limit of the rotifers studied lies above that of most bacteria but below that of the larger algae the same species of rotifer becomes predominantly a herbivore in oligotrophic waters but a member of the decomposer trophic group in eutrophic waters. This example should at least discourage broad generalizations about the trophic role of whole groups of organisms and over a wide range of communities.

5.4.4 The influence of internal physiological factors on digestive efficiency

With increasing knowledge of the feeding efficiency of laboratory animals it is becoming clear that much of the individual variation which exists is attributable to factors such as moulting, ripening of gonads and other processes which are related to age, development or season. However, very little systematic study has yet been made on invertebrates and only two examples from small mammals will be mentioned here. Evans (1968) has reported some of the complicated interactions between seasonal changes in food quality (especially the increased protein content of grasses during the spring 'flush') and pregnancy and lactation in the vole *Microtus agrestis*. In the male the spring flush is accompanied by an increase in body protein but this is delayed in the female which normally has two litters during the year. In the first litter numbers are lower and survival is less good than in the later litter despite the fact that the first lactation coincides with highest nutritive value in the grass. This is the more surprising because Trojan (1968) found in *Microtus arvalis* that lactation increases the cost of maintenance by twice as much as does pregnancy (20 per cent instead of 10 per cent).

5.4.5 Examples of the determination of assimilation efficiency from the ratio of faeces to consumption

For the reasons already given, calculation of assimilation is difficult and its direct measurement impossible. The most obvious method of determining assimilation/consumption ratio is by difference: that is to say, since $A = C - (F + U)$, we determine C and $F + U$ and we calculate:

$$\frac{C - (F + U)}{C} = \frac{A}{C} \qquad \qquad 5.7$$

This has been quite widely done for captive animals, large and small. Faeces are collected, dried and weighed and food consumption is determined by difference. Since many foods loose water on exposure it may be necessary to expose control samples under similar conditions to those experienced by the food which is supplied to the animal and to allow for such losses.

In vertebrate studies, when it is not possible to collect all the faeces, Edin's (1926) method of labelling food with an indigestible tracer (usually chromic oxide) can be applied. If the food supplied to the animal is metered (and the total quantity of tracer taken up daily can thus be estimated) and if it is assumed that the same quantity is excreted daily in the faeces, then measurements of the strength of tracer in the faeces permit calculation of the total quantity produced daily (see Milner, 1967).

An example of the calculation of assimilation/consumption ratios for an invertebrate in the laboratory is provided by Wiegert's (1965) studies of grasshoppers. These were kept in cages, given ample food supplies and the grass consumption and faeces production were measured over three day periods. Some idea of the variability encountered in such work can be gained from his figures which show efficiencies from 24 per cent to 53 per cent for nine individuals of one species and from 21 per cent to 64 per cent for seven individuals of another species. Such variability appears to be very common. Taken in conjunction with the difficulties of extrapolating from laboratory conditions to the field, they render such estimates of assimilation/consumption efficiency of very doubtful value as a means of comparing the performance of, say, one grasshopper with another. However, this is probably an extreme example; greater precision is certainly possible when measurements are replicated and account is taken of factors enumerated in the above sections. At least the discrepancy between major phyla, such as insects on the one hand and mammals on the other, is usually so great that even quite crude estimates are of some value as a warning against generalising too widely throughout the whole animal kingdom (Wiegert and Evans, 1967). Also rather consistent discrepancies do appear to be the general rule between the efficiencies of different trophic types. For instance, Balogh (1958b) has drawn attention to this phenomenon, particularly in the case of herbivores, carnivores and detritus feeders, which show consistent differences according to their type of food.

6

The Study of Respiration and Energy Flow in Relation to Secondary Production

6.0 Introduction

As has already been mentioned (see 1.3), work on the production of secondary consumers contributes to ecological understanding in three major fields of enquiry which have, until recently, been pursued separately.

The first field involves measuring the amount of growth of which a population is capable under realistic conditions, measuring the effects on production of changes in internal and external factors and of different regimes of predation and harvesting. Such work is the necessary theoretical basis for efficient practical exploitation of natural and domesticated populations and the previous sections cover essential techniques of population analysis and demographic study.

The second and third fields, those of production ecology linked to the study of energy flow, are concerned with understanding, comparing and analysing the functional properties of whole ecosystems and of their component parts. In the first field we are interested in respiration (or metabolism) as an item of the energy budget of the individual or the population which reduces the production/assimilation efficiency; in the second and third types of study it is more frequently used as an index of assimilation when making comparisons between rival populations exploiting a similar resource, when comparing trophic groups one with another, or when contrasting major food webs or ecosystems.

In detailed investigations on a single species the influence of environmental conditions, life cycle stage, etc. on respiratory rate (and its share of assimilation) must be measured carefully. In studies which cover the hundreds of different species that occur together in an ecosystem such detailed analysis is not possible and various assumptions and simplifications must be made if any progress is to be achieved. Typical of such simplications are:
(a) the calculation of specific respiratory (metabolic) rates, as units of respiration (metabolism) per gramme of body weight or, better, on the

assumption that a power law relationship to body weight applies. Weights may, in turn, be related to linear measurements.

(b) the calculation of a single coefficient of respiratory (metabolic) rate per unit of biomass with the direct conversion from biomass per unit area to respiration rate (metabolism).

(c) similar direct relationships may be assumed between numbers and respiration rate.

(d) the assumption that a specific respiratory rate factor, determined on one species, is applicable to the entire population regardless of age, sex or other demographic group and/or to a wider taxonomic group than the species on which the measurements were made.

(e) the use of overall respiration/temperature factors or the acceptance of assumptions about diurnal or annual temperature regimes and their effects on respiration rate.

(f) the use of respiration data derived from one population, habitat or ecosystem, in conjunction with census and demographic data derived from other populations.

All these practices have been widely employed, often with little attempt to measure the errors involved and would clearly be indefensible in studies of the first kind. In preliminary surveys of whole ecosystems for which we may lack even precise census data, however we frequently have the alternatives of using inadequate criteria such as the above or abandoning the attempt to employ energy flow analysis altogether.

The insight gained from the work, for instance, of Odum and his colleagues on a range of diverse ecosystems from freshwater springs to coral reefs, salt marshes and old fields would appear to justify the attempt to employ such data in preliminary surveys.

In the sections which follow we attempt to survey a very large field. After a preliminary discussion on the principles of respiration (or metabolism) measurement we consider in turn: measurements on individual animals in the laboratory, factors which influence the application of these results to laboratory populations, direct measurements for use on populations in the field and fourthly the synthesis of field population data with laboratory metabolism measurements. Finally, some results obtained so far are discussed especially in as much as they throw light on respiration/assimilation ratios.

6.1 Laboratory respiration measurements on individual animals

6.1.1 Principles

'*La réspiration est donc une combustion*'. (Lavoisier, 1780.)

Combustion is a physical process which can be measured in terms of heat liberated or chemical exchanges taking place. In the case of aerobic respiration, the latter involve oxygen uptake and carbon dioxide liberation and these are quantitatively related to heat liberation for each particular food substance. Thus, if the combusted substances are known, the measurement of one of the three variables defines the remaining two. In the case of pure organic compounds the heat output is simply related to the quantity of carbon according to the values given in Table D in the Appendix (see p. 160).

The relation between the number of molecules (and thus, in a perfect gas, of volumes) of carbon dioxide evolved and of oxygen absorbed is termed the respiratory quotient ('R.Q.'). It may be calculated from the percentage composition of the elements in the compound being eaten. In the case of carbohydrates the gas volumes are (for all practical purposes) equal and R.Q. equals 1.

In the case of fats the value is around 0·71 and in proteins it is around 0·80 respectively.

Thus, when working to accuracy levels normal in physiology, either the food composition must be known or else two of the three quantities (oxygen input, carbon dioxide output or heat evolution) must be measured. Since, however, the oxygen uptake associated with liberation of one calorie varies only ±5% over the full range of normal foodstuffs, for many ecological purposes no correction in relation to respiratory quotient is needed to account for variations in the food substances contained in the diet.

Carbon dioxide evolution, on the other hand, varies by about ±10% and is thus more subject to influence by the foodstuffs concerned.

In sections 6.1.2, 6.1.3 and 6.1.4 the main methods for measuring heat output, oxygen consumption and carbon dioxide output will be reviewed briefly and their different applications indicated. Sketches of the main types of respirometer appear in Fig. 6.5. The common feature which applies to all metabolic measurements must first be mentioned, however: namely the basis on which results are to be expressed.

Two distinct approaches to the measurement of population metabolism are possible. In ecological work which is aimed at the synthesis of activity of whole populations, respiration or heat production measurements may be made on whole populations, or at least mass collections of individuals *provided that* the composition and conditions of existence in the experiments are comparable with those in the field. In work of an analytical nature, on the other hand, and when the effects of different population structures, age, class, composition, etc. must be measured, it is clearly essential that measurements should be made on a single individual organism at a time because there is usually great variation between individuals and this variation is best related to such factors as size, age, condition, sex, etc. Thus the primary data usually take the form of metabolic units per individual per unit of time. In more approximate work of the second and third categories of part 6.0 (General energy flow studies) it may be advantageous to convert this information into metabolic units per unit weight—per g or per kg as convenient. In this way the metabolic rate of whole populations can be readily obtained from total biomass data. However, such a practice presupposes a linear relationship between individual weight and metabolism whereas, as discussed in sections 5.0 and 6.2.3, this relationship is almost never linear and usually approximates to:

$$a = W^{\frac{3}{4}} \dotfill 6.1$$

There has been much controversy over the exact value of the exponent in this equation but current opinion is predominantly in favour of the value of 0·75 for reasons which are discussed very fully in Kleiber (1961), Bertallanfy (1957b) and Brody (1945). The practical effects of this relationship are that the metabolic rate of a mammal is about 70 $W^{\frac{3}{4}}$ kcal/day/kg and that a graph of body weight against logarithm of metabolic rate is a straight line (Fig. 6.1).

Calculations from population biomass give, thus, only a crude first approximation to population metabolism. This was found to be the case for a population of Harvestmen by Phillipson (1963).

When a unit of biomass or weight of standing crop is required it is possible to use the crude live weight of the animal, its dry weight or some index of its protoplasm content. It is often possible to determine regression equations interrelating these, but a number of sources of variation must be borne in mind. Live weights, especially in the case of mammalian herbivores, can be greatly influenced by the weight of the gut content, both of food and of water. It may be desirable to make measurements at a standard time of day

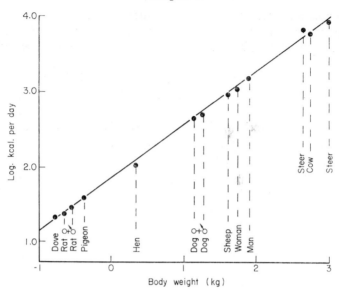

Figure 6.1. Relationship between weight and metabolic rate over a range of vertebrates (After Kleiber, 1961). Abscissa=body weight in kg. Ordinate=metabolism in log kcal per day.

or season or to remove the gut contents in the case of dead animals. In the case of small mammals variability can usually be reduced by making numerous measurements. A further consideration which applies especially to comparisons between species is the variation in water content and of heavy non-living skeletal material in some animals. Zeuthen (1947) for instance, in comparing a range of marine invertebrates, some of which had heavy shells, measured their nitrogen content by Kjeldahl analysis and expressed all weights in terms of protein nitrogen presumed to be incorporated in the protoplasm.

The further requirement for standardization may arise in connection with the state of activity of the organism. It is usual to find that, when first placed in a small laboratory respirometer, animals show especially high metabolic rates. When experiments are prolonged on the other hand the rate falls off as a result of starvation. As a result, most investigators ignore metabolism occurring during the initial period of enhanced activity and a later period of food shortage, and concentrate their attention on the period between. Large mammal respirometers may contain exercise wheels and other devices permitting an approach to more normal activity rhythms and also food supplies. Workers with invertebrates have often investigated the effect of anaesthesia to see to what extent the activity of animals in the respirometer is above a certain 'basic' rate (e.g. Nielsen, 1949). The whole question of 'basic' and 'standard' metabolic rates (see Brody, 1945) is subject to question at the present time, especially by the ecologist who is unable to relate these to field activity.

A useful approach to small mammal metabolism measurement is due to Polish workers who distinguish average daily metabolic rate (ADMR) which can be measured in a respirometer under optimal conditions and related to the weight of an animal on the one hand, from metabolism related to thermo-regulation (also measured under controlled conditions on a specific animal) on the other hand. These can be added together to give a daily energy budget (DEB) which provides a reliable prediction of the performance of animals under field conditions (see Górecki and Grodziński, 1968). Further modifications to DEB can be made to allow for such factors as pregnancy and lactation which increase it and behaviour such as huddling together in the nest which reduces it.

Sometimes there is evidence for the persistence of considerable endogenous rhythms in a respirometer (Macfadyen, 1961; Fig. 6.2) but this only makes one suspect that the uniform conditions which obtain in most apparatus may suppress metabolic variations which would otherwise occur under more natural conditions. In fact there is an urgent need for apparatus permitting measurement of metabolic rates under non-uniform conditions: a need which has only been met to a small extent by respirometers but which may soon instead be satisfied by one of the tracer methods (section 6.3.2).

6.1.2 Calorimetry

Calorimetry is, in some ways, the most fundamental method of metabolism measurement because heat output is a direct expression of energy liberation from food. However, despite a great deal of work (Swietoslawski, 1946; Calvet and Prat, 1956, 1963) the equipment involved is usually more complex and the results less reliable than those obtained by other methods. A funda-mental and particularly intractable problem in the use of calorimetry is the large amount of heat which is associated with the vaporisation of water. Since most animals require relatively humid surroundings and respire water vapour when they metabolise, it is difficult to prevent an inbalance between

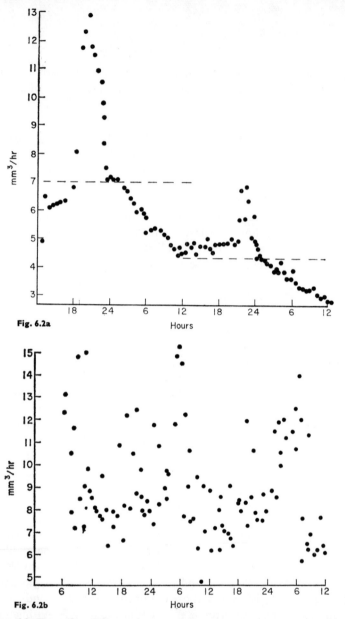

Fig. 6.2a

Fig. 6.2b

Figure 6.2. Examples of the persistence of diurnal respiratory rhythms obtained by using a continuous recording respirometer. Peaks in respiration are consistent with peaks in a field activity. The first figure relates to *Platybunus triangularis* (Opiliones) shown by Williams (1962) to exhibit climbing activity at dusk; the second figure refers to the woodlouse *Oniscus asellus* which is most active just before dawn.

evaporation and condensation in the calorimeter. This involves the uptake of some 536 calories per gram of water — an amount of heat which may well mask that derived from metabolism.

Calorimeters for mammals and other large animals are quite feasible, but require total enclosure; they usually involve measurement of temperature rise in a flow of water through a jacket which surrounds the animal cage. Calibration is best performed by liberating a known quantity of heat from an electrical resistance using the relation that 4·18 Joules = 1 calorie. An alternative approach involves the use of a second, control, calorimeter with an automatic mechanism which adjusts the rate of gain of heat to be equal in the two chambers (Hawkins, 1958). In such large calorimeters the heat involved in evaporation of water is best arrived at by condensing all the water from the air stream and calculating the implied heat loss.

Calorimeters have been used for invertebrates but not widely adopted for the reasons given above: perhaps the best likelihood of future development in this direction lies in continuous flow methods with compensation, exploiting the great sensitivity of thermistors and present day amplifiers. This approach is being made by several workers and commercial equipment has been developed in Sweden by the firm of L.K.B.

In certain special cases there is the possibility of using calorimetry in populations as they occur in nature. This will be discussed in section 6.3.3.

6.1.3 Oxygen consumption

For the reasons given in section 6.1.1 oxygen consumption measurements are a better index of energy liberation when the diet is unknown than are measurements of carbon dioxide output. They are, in fact, the preferred method of metabolic measurement in most cases.

6.1.3.1 *Analytical methods*
In order to detect the uptake of oxygen by an animal it must be retained in a confined space. The depletion of oxygen can then be measured by the successive analysis of the oxygen of the confined air. This can be done by withdrawing samples and determining the oxygen absorbed by means of Pyrogallol or by the Winkler method. Continuous monitoring of oxygen content is also possible by means of the oxygen electrode and by measurement of the magnetic properties of the air (oxygen is highly diamagnetic). All these methods of oxygen content measurement have been used but none are highly sensitive (see Table 6.1). The oxygen electrode, for instance, has a

considerable oxygen uptake by itself: magnetic measurements require large samples and the Pyrogallol method is very difficult to use with small volumes.

The vast majority of oxygen uptake methods depend instead on manometric procedures. In these methods it is necessary to absorb the carbon dioxide given by the organisms so that, when it takes in oxygen, the total amount of gas in the chamber is reduced. The rate of uptake is then measured through the reduction in either the volume or the pressure of the air in the animal chamber or from a combination of these.

6.1.3.2 *Constant volume methods*

The classical constant volume respirometer is the Warburg apparatus (see Fig. 6.5, No. 1 and Umbreit *et al.*, 1957). In this the vessel is connected to a manometer and the volume of the vessel plus part of the adjacent manometer limb (which is partly filled with an aqueous solution) is kept constant by varying the pressure on the distal (open) limb of the manometer. Changes of pressure needed to keep the volume constant are related to oxygen uptake by calculations, for which the flask volume and other information are needed.

The Warburg respirometer has been used for longer than almost any piece of physiological apparatus but its days are probably numbered, at least for long term respirometry because despite its great merit of simplicity it is sensitive to outside pressure changes, requires regular attention for readings and is tedious to calibrate.

6.1.3.3 *Compensating respirometers*

The problem of sensitivity to pressure change is overcome in compensating respirometers in which a second flask is connected to the 'open' end of the Warburg manometer. This involves a halving of sensitivity but results in great improvements in stability. In the early versions, such as the Barcroft respirometer (1908) the oxygen uptake was calculated from the change in relative height of fluid in the U tube; some sensitivity was regained by using a light fluid such as kerosene and a narrow tube. An improvement, probably first introduced by Dixon (1937, 1951) and also attributed to many other authors involves restoration of the index mark to a constant position by replacing the gas removed in respiration with some kind of piston in a side tube (Fig. 6.5, No. 2). The 'piston' in these earlier forms was a column of mercury or other liquid; in later versions such as those described by Scholander (1942, 1950) and Davies (1966), a solid rod is driven by a micrometer screw (Fig. 6.3). In all such cases the oxygen taken up is directly replaced by

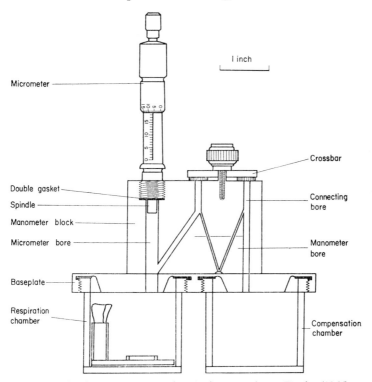

Figure 6.3. Scholander type compensating respirometer due to Davies (1966).

movement of the piston and this can be measured very accurately. A recent version of this type of respirometer is now available commercially known as the Gilson respirometer and would appear to have great possibilities as a practical laboratory instrument.

An alternative to mechanical compensation for gas loss in this last type of respirometer is the direct replacement of oxygen itself. This has the obvious advantage that the oxygen/nitrogen ratio remains constant and the system is readily adaptable for continuous automatic recording. Attempts have been made to supply the oxygen from a reservoir but the more usual method is to do this by electrolysis. This idea has a long history going back for at least fifty years (see Macfadyen, 1961). In most versions (Fig. 6.5, No. 3) the advantage of isolation from the atmosphere is lost because electrolytic generation of oxygen is accompanied by generation of hydrogen which must

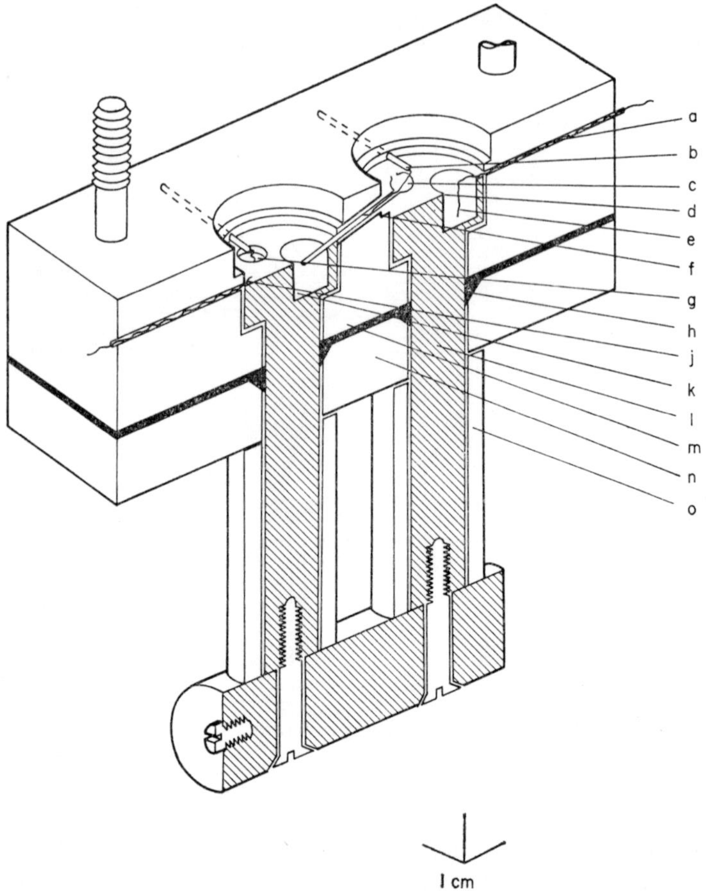
a
b
c
d
e
f
g
h
j
k
l
m
n
o
1 cm

Figure 6.4. Electrolytic recording respirometer after Macfadyen (1961). (a) Connection to oxygen generator in compensating vessel. (b) Connection to pressure electrode. (c) Glass bulb holding pressure electrode in place. (d) Plated rod forming floor to compensating chamber. (e) Oxygen generator (containing $CuSO_4$) in compensating chamber. (f) Meniscus used to detect pressure change. (g) Oxygen generator in animal chamber. (h) Rubber O-ring. (j) Connection for thermistor. (k) Alkali vessel in animal chamber. (l) Copper rod (for thermal equilibration). (m) Plastic body (impact resistant polystyrene)—upper part. (n) Plastic body (impact resistant polystyrene)—lower part. (o) Perspex sleeve (insulation).

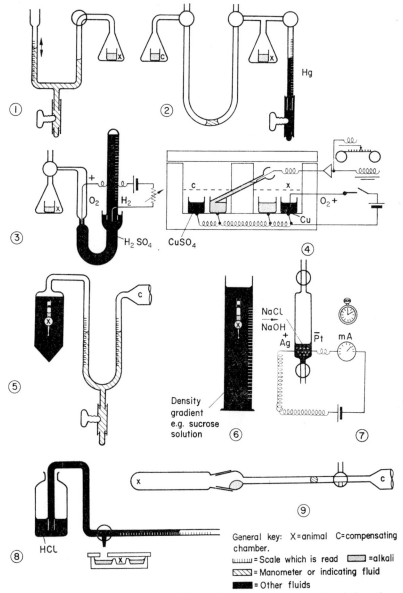

Figure 6.5. Summary sketches of the main types of respirometer (other than calorimeters).

List of types illustrated:

1. Constant volume Warburg—open.
2. Compensating respirometer with mechanical restoration.
3. Simple electrolytic respirometer—open.
4. Compensating automatic respirometer.
5. Cartesian diver respirometer.
6. Gradient diver respirometer.
7. Köpf's method of carbon dioxide determination.
8. Conway micro-diffusion method.
9. Constant pressure respirometer. As improved by Llewellyn.

Chapter 6

be liberated from the system if pressure is not to build up. (This is true of respirometers by Swaby and Passey, 1953, Winteringham, 1959, and Phillipson, 1962). Two ways of avoiding this have been adopted; the absorption of hydrogen by palladium (Wager and Porter, 1961) and the production of copper or other metal instead of hydrogen as in the respirometer of Macfadyen (1961) (Fig. 6.4 and Fig. 6.5, No. 4). In the latter case copper sulphate is electrolised.

$$CuSO_4 \longrightarrow Cu^= + SO_4^{++}$$
$$SO_4 + H_2O \longrightarrow \tfrac{1}{2} O_2 + H_2SO_4$$

By retaining a manometrically closed system, complete symmetry is achieved and this type of respirometer offers, for the first time, the possibility of subjecting the system to temperature changes during experiments and thus of overcoming one of the major problems mentioned in section 6.1.1. Although some progress has been made in this direction (for instance, Fourche (1967) has successfully worked with *Drosophila* eggs) the method has not yet been fully developed.

6.1.3.4 *Constant pressure respirometers*

Probably the simplest type of manometric respirometer possible is the constant pressure instrument which, until recently has been strangely neglected. In this case the animal chamber containing also a carbon dioxide absorbent is connected to a capillary tube which is calibrated in absolute volume units (Fig. 6.5, No. 9). A drop of marker fluid introduced to the distal end of the calibrated tube moves towards the animal chamber as the oxygen is used up; no calibration is required. Changes in external pressure can be compensated by the use of a control manometer or by connection through a manifold to a 'dummy atmosphere' (consisting of a large airtight vessel) (Llewellyn *in litt.*). The whole must, of course, be kept in a water bath, but for many purposes it is better that this should not be thermostatically controlled; it should simply be kept gently stirred in a room of approximately the same temperature as the experiment.

This method has been used by Wiegert (1965) and other American authors with success and has recently been improved with the result that sensitivities of better than 0·1 μl O_2/hr have readily been obtained.

6.1.3.5 *Cartesian Diver Respirometers*

The diver respirometer does not necessarily operate either at constant volume or at constant pressure; it is the most sensitive method available and has been greatly extended in recent years. A full account of this method is not possible here; for general principles and theory the reader is referred to papers by Linderstrøm-Lang (1943) and Holter (1943).

In the diver respirometer (Fig. 6.5, No. 5) the respiring organism is contained within a small glass float together with some alkali and a short column of salt solution which is continuous with the surrounding flotation medium. The float is normally submerged in the medium within a closed vessel which is connected to a water manometer. Reduction in gas volume causes the salt solution to enter the diver neck which thus becomes heavier. The pressure on the whole system (diver and floatation medium) is controlled by the manometer which is at first adjusted so that the diver is buoyant enough to remain exactly suspended in the medium. On successive occasions the reduction in pressure necessary to prevent the diver from sinking is determined and from the changes in pressure in the manometer the gas volume reduction can be calculated.

Among many later improvements of potential interest to ecologists are the development of stoppered divers which need no calibration and are better adapted to confining and releasing animals (Zeuthen, 1950, 1964). Secondly, the demountable diver (Gregg and Linz, 1967) has been developed for larger species and thirdly the gradient diver method has been developed in which the diver sinks slowly through a solution of increasing density (Fig. 6.5, No. 6); this permits continuous recording (Løville and Zeuthen, 1962; Lints, Lints and Zeuthen, 1967). Finally, two methods have been described in which the buoyancy of the diver is balanced by controlled electromagnetic forces. This permits the use of the diver as an automatic respirometer (Brzin *et al.*, 1965; Lovtrup and Larson, 1965).

The great advantages of the diver type respirometer are its extreme sensitivity (down to 10^{-6} µl/hr oxygen uptake) and its cheapness in terms of purchaseable equipment. This is not necessarily true in terms of skilled labour, however. The chief disadvantage for most types of respirometry with whole terrestrial animals are the conditions to which the animal is subjected; for it is placed in a very small chamber at very strictly maintained temperatures. In addition, operation demands great skill and until recently automatic reading has not been possible. This objection has now been met as mentioned above.

In general then oxygen consumption methods are available which cover the full range of sensitivity required for animal respirometry. Most of these, however, involve confinement in very unnatural physical conditions and require skilled operation and constant attention. Given the latter, excellent results can be and have been obtained although there is still an urgent need for further development of respirometers specifically for use by ecologists and which meet the objections raised above.

6.1.4   Carbon dioxide evolution

As already explained the measurement of carbon dioxide evolution by itself is perhaps the least useful index of metabolic rate. However, in conjunction with the measurement of oxygen consumption it permits the calculation of respiratory quotients and as a crude measure of metabolic rate some carbon dioxide methods have the advantage of much greater simplicity.

Methods can once again be classed as analytical or manometric.

6.1.4.1   *Analytical methods*

In this case the analytical methods have been more widely used than mano-metric and by far the commonest principle is the absorption of carbon dioxide in alkali solution and measurement of chemical change therein. Absorption in alkali may require bubbling of gas through the solution as in the Petenkoffer apparatus (see James and James, 1940), entrainment of gas between circulating bubbles together with continuous automatic analysis or by simple solution following diffusion of the gas (Conway, 1950; Elkan and Moore, 1962). See Fig. 6.5, No. 8.

A great many methods of analysis have been used including electrical measurement of conductivity and pH, colour change in indicators, back titration of the alkali against acid, and the use of the so-called carbon dioxide electrode (a modified glass electrode attached to a pH meter (Jensen *et al.*, 1966)).

When titration is to be carried out and indicators are used the preferred method is either to absorb the carbon dioxide in barium hydroxide, or, better, to use sodium or potassium hydroxide and to add an excess of barium chloride before titrating. The reason for this is that the alkali-metal carbonates interfere with the action of phenolphthalein and similar indicators; and must therefore be precipitated. In the case of absorption in potassium hydroxide by diffusion, the barium chloride cannot be added to the alkali before exposure because, if this is done, a 'scum' of carbonate crystals forms on the absorbing surface and prevents diffusion of the gas and greatly decreases the absorption rate.

It is not essential to absorb carbon dioxide in alkali; it can be absorbed in deionized water, and the change in conductivity or in pH is then measured (James, 1964; Bowman, 1968).

In an ingenious method devised by Köpf (1952) carbon dioxide is absorbed in salt solution (sodium chloride N/10) which contains phenolphthalein (Fig. 6.5, No. 7). The acidity resulting from the carbon dioxide is compensated by electrolytic generation of alkali at a platinum cathode as follows:

$$NaCl \longrightarrow Na^- + Cl^+$$
$$Na^- + H_2O \longrightarrow NaOH + \tfrac{1}{2}H_2$$

The chlorine is absorbed on a silver anode and forms silver chloride; it can be removed again by reversing the current.

The total electric charge (in coulombs) needed to maintain the pH of the salt solution (as indicated by the phenolphthalein) is a direct measure of carbon dioxide absorbed. This method has since been developed for analysis of small samples of a few millilitres (Macfadyen, in prep.).

6.1.4.2 *Manometric methods*

Manometric methods of carbon dioxide production have really only been used in conjunction with the measurement of oxygen uptake. Clearly if the two measurements can be combined in a single experiment this is a great advantage for determining R.Q. because respiratory quotients can be calculated from a single experiment. The usual methods are those employed in Warburg respirometry. In the 'direct method' a normal Warburg experiment (involving absorption of carbon dioxide in alkali) is carried out simultaneously with a second experiment in which no carbon dioxide is absorbed. From the difference in volume change between the paired experiments any departure from a 1 to 1 gas volume change can be detected. In this method the flask containing alkali is kept without carbon dioxide whilst the other flask accumulates progressively more of this gas. The unequal levels of carbon dioxide may well influence the results and for this reason the 'indirect method' was introduced by Warburg and the carbon dioxide buffer method of Pardee was developed. Both these methods are fully described and discussed by Umbreit *et al.* (1957).

Chapter 6

6.1.5 Comparison of the sensitivity and use of different methods of respiration measurement

In the light of the previous discussion it may be useful to have a summary of the uses and performance data of a range of typical respirometers. This is given in table 6.1.

6.2 Factors affecting the application of respiration measurements to laboratory populations

6.2.1 Factors to which respiration data must be related

Conventional laboratory determinations of metabolic rate, based on individual organisms collected randomly are notoriously variable. This can be seen from the examination of almost any published data on respiration rates. This variability can be due to factors which are peculiar to the individual organism; its age, sex, stage of development, condition in relation to cycles of growth and moulting or to individual variations in genotype. It can be due to factors influenced by the relationship of the individual to the rest of the species population of which it is part; this reflects the effects of crowding, social factors and other intraspecific interactions. It can be due to interaction with other species, including especially those on which it depends for food but also those which, by parasitising it and by preying upon it, have a profound influence on its behaviour and energy budget. Finally, of course, variability can be due to factors in the physical and climatic environment such as temperature, humidity, osmotic pressure and respiratory gas composition which normally vary both in space and time.

Nearly all these factors can be manipulated and most of them can be held constant in the laboratory. If we are to relate laboratory data to field conditions, the influence of such factors, should, in theory, be investigated in every case. In practice this is hardly possible at present time; the importance of such effects must therefore be assessed by the ecologist who will usually select only those which are likely to dominate a given situation. In order to provide some background of experience, examples of different effects are reviewed in the following sections (6.2.2 to 6.2.4).

6.2.2 The influence of population factors on respiration rate

The most direct effect of population size on metabolism obviously acts through the availability of food: when the population is overcrowded, food

TABLE 6.1. Comparison of performance of Respirometers.

(1) Respirometer	(2) Measures O₂,CO₂, cals	(3) Container volume ml	(4) Normal rates µl/hr	(5) Normal accuracy	(6) Automation	(7) Sensitivity: smallest detectable change (µl)
WARBURG Normal	O_2 and CO_2	25	10–500	2 µl/hr	N	0·5
Small vessels	O_2 and CO_2	5	2–50	1 µl/hr	N	0·5
GILSON Normal	O_2 and CO_2	16	5–500	2 µl/hr	P	0·5
DIVER Holter	O_2 and CO_2	0·005–0·05	0·01–1·0	5%	P	0·0001
Gregg and Lints	O_2 and CO_2	0·005–0·05	0·01–1·0	5%	Y	0·005
Gradient	O_2 and CO_2	0·001–0·05	0·01–1·0	3%	Y	0·0001
PHILLIPSON automatic	O_2 and CO_2	50	50–300	8%	Y	10
MACFADYEN electrolytic	O_2 and CO_2	7	1–100	1 µl/hr	Y	0·01
FENN, etc. capillary const. vol.	O_2	1·0	2·0 ca	5%	P	0·05
LLEWELLYN et al. const. pressure	O_2	1–10	0·1–5	2%	N	0·05
CONWAY microdiffusion	CO_2	20	50–1000+	20 µl/hr	N	20
JENSEN CO_2 diffusion	CO_2	10	1·0 ca	0·05 µl/hr	Y	—
CALVET microcalorimeter	heat	15–100	20–1000+	1%	Y	0·2
WINKLER (dissolved oxygen)	O_2	10	100 ca	2%	N	30

Notes: All quantities are converted to equivalents of oxygen volumes, regardless of the parameter actually measured.

(5) Accuracy is expressed as the expected standard error of a series of readings over the normal range or, where accuracy declines at low ranges, as the probable minimum detectable rate.

(6) The column 'Automation' indicates whether application of automatic recording is possible (Y), inherently impossible (N), or potentially possible (P).

and hence energy supplies become scarce, and starvation reduces the amount of metabolism which is possible. In starvation, the extent to which survival is reduced is only approximately proportional to the deficiency in calories, but survival of warm-blooded animals is extended or reduced when energy loss from heat is increased or decreased by manipulation of the environmental temperature. Thus, Kleiber (1961) reports experiments in which starved rats survived for eleven days at 20°C and for seventeen days at 30°C. However, the total metabolism involved in these two cases is not the same: the rat survives and uses up more of its initial energy supplies before death, when kept at a warmer level. In fact most mammals have a critical temperature, below which extra heat is required for survival and which is disproportionately decreased. Above the critical temperature excess heat is produced, despite the fact that it is not needed for temperature regulation.

Under less extreme conditions the effects of population pressure on metabolism must largely operate through behavioural factors. Much work has been done on the effect of social hierarchy and similar factors on the chances of survival and of reproduction of the individuals concerned. At present almost nothing seems to have been published on the effect of such factors on metabolic activity. An indication of probable importance of such factors is to be found in the work of Kawanabe (1958, 1959) in which it is demonstrated that the position of a fish in the social hierarchy (itself in consequence of crowding) directly determines its rate of growth. Another effect of density on metabolism is suggested by Green's (1964) work on the spacing behaviour of the Springtail, *Folsomia candida*. Green found that these animals, possibly through a pheromone-like subsistence, normally maintained a spacing of a few body widths from each other. When the density is such as to permit 'optimum' spacing, reproductive activity is at maximum and movement at a minimum. At other densities the animals spent much time moving around.

A most extreme form of influence of social factors on metabolism is to be found amongst the locusts. In this group the solitary and gregarious animals, although genotypically the same, exhibit such extreme differences in metabolic activity as virtually to resemble different species (Faure, 1932). Yet other examples of a similar nature are to be found amongst the tent caterpillars which are pests of Canadian spruce trees (Wellington, 1960).

6.2.3 The influence of life cycle factors on respiration rate

In general, specific metabolic rate (rate per unit of weight) decreases with age and increasing weight during an animal's lifetime. This relationship approaches the form

$$R = W^{0.75} \dotfill 6.2$$

as has already been discussed (see 5.0). However, the weight of animal is rarely an exactly predictable function of age, and, naturally, it depends upon environmental and other factors. Careful studies usually show regular and irregular departures from a smooth metabolism/age curve. When the mean metabolic activity of an entire population is studied in relation to the whole developmental period, it is found that consistent departures from a smooth relationship do occur. A useful example of such a study, which refers to *Tribolium castaneum*, the flour beetle, is given by Klekowski, Prus and Żyromska-Rudzka (1967). These authors found that from the second to the final larval stages there was a linear relationship between the logarithm of oxygen consumption and the logarithm of weight. However, both younger and older animals had specific metabolic rates which were about ten times lower: the egg being lowest of all followed by pupa, adult and first larvae (Fig. 6.6).

When the metabolic rate of the single individual is related to age by the means of a linear graph, the result is as shown in Fig. 6.7. That is to say there is a more or less exponential increase in metabolism from the first to the sixth larval instar followed by a dramatic decline in the seventh larval, pre-pupal and early pupal instars. This is followed by a small rise just before hatching and then a continued rather low level through adult life, the female being somewhat more active than the male.

Equally remarkable variations in metabolic activity, in relation to age, instar and sexual development have been detected in other invertebrates. Wieser (1962) demonstrated marked increases in metabolic activity of isopod crustacea at the time of moulting and Phillipson (1967b) reports a similar effect in the *Polydesmus angustus* when immature. In this study, the effect of ripening gonads on metabolic activity is also apparent. The same author (Phillipson, 1963) has also demonstrated a particularly large increase in metabolism association with reproductive activity in the opilionid, *Leiobunum rotundum*.

Among the more primitive arthropods, some information about the relation between metabolic activity and age is available for oribatid mites and for Collembola. With regard to the latter, Healey (1965, 1967) found that 100 µg adult individuals of *Onychiurus procampatus* consumed $32 \cdot 10^{-3}$ µl of oxygen

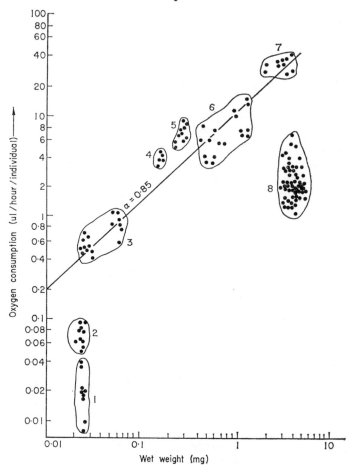

Figure 6.6. Relation between weight and metabolism in *Tribolium castaneum* (After Klekowski, Prus and Żyromska-Rudzka, 1967). 1=eggs, 2=larvae I, 3=larvae II, 4=larvae III, 5=larvae IV, 6=larvae V, 7=larvae VI, 8=prepupae, pupae and adults.

per hour. Young specimens of $\frac{1}{10}$ of the weight consumed $\frac{1}{3}$ of this quantity. No departures from a steady decline in specific activity with age were detected by this author. Webb (1968) on the other hand working especially with *Platynothrus peltifer* found the highest specific activity in the deuttonymphal stage, both the adult and younger stages being less active.

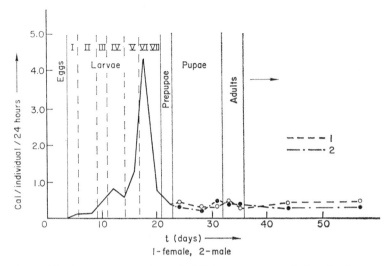

Figure 6.7. Oxygen consumption of *Tribolium castaneum* during development (in calories per individual; 1=female, 2=male).

Amongst mammals the effect of age on metabolic rate is not amenable to simple generalisation: the rat, for instance, behaves differently from man (Kleiber, 1961, chapter 11). In the rat the metabolic rate increases steadily throughout life, although the rate of increase is lower after puberty. The specific rate per unit of weight is at a maximum soon after birth while the rate per unit of surface area has a minimum at about one-third of the maximum life span and rises steadily thereafter. In man, on the other hand, there is a steady decline in the latter statistics and perhaps the most conspicuous feature in this species is the much higher metabolic rate per individual for the male than for the female in adolescence. The seventeen year old man metabolises at about 1,700 kcal/day against the women's 1,400. These rates decline in such a way that they converge at an age of about seventy years.

It is clear, therefore, that amongst the many groups of animals only the crudest estimates of population metabolism are to be derived from spot determinations of the metabolic activity of individuals if these have not been related to such factors as have been discussed in this section. Any serious attempts to derive the true energy budget for a species must be based on numerous readings arranged to cover the full range of life stage, age and season as well as both sexes.

6.2.4 The influence of factors in the physical environment on respiration rate

The majority of laboratory metabolic rate determinations have been made with remarkably little concern for the effect of physical factors on respiration. This is despite the fact that such factors are well known to determine respiration rate over a wide range. From the point of view of many experiments the main reason for controlling temperature of a respirometer would appear to have been, not so much the desire to control the animal's environment as to control that of the apparatus and to prevent spurious readings. The latter is, of course, essential but so too is the former, as will be seen from the following points.

(a) Although constant environmental conditions lead to abnormal behaviour (e.g. Cloudsley-Thompson, 1951a, 1951b, 1953), most experiments are conducted under constant temperature conditions.

(b) Very great and, far from simple, consequences follow temperature changes whether these occur rapidly or slowly. (Cf. Grainger, 1956, 1958, and Bertnet, 1964.)

(c) Although carbon dioxide levels have an important influence on respiration rates the level in most respirometers is maintained at zero.

(d) Although many invertebrates and microbes cannot tolerate desiccation, many experiments are conducted in the presence of strong alkali which have the effect of maintaining relative humidities well below levels which are tolerable.

(e) Although not strictly relevant under this heading, there is a further complication that many quite simple animals exhibit behaviour patterns such as clustering together, maintaining definite distances from each other and so on. When isolated or overcrowded such forms are abnormally active or inactive and must certainly produce spurious data. One example of this is Green's (1964) demonstration of spacing activity in *Folsomia candida* already referred to (see section 2.2.2).

Factors of this kind are usually ignored by experimenters when conducting this type of experiment.

In general, the physical factor which has the greatest influence on metabolism is temperature. Most chemical reactions follow Van't Hoff's law, according to which

$$V = AK^t \dots\dots\dots\dots\dots\dots\dots\dots\dots\dots\dots\dots\dots\dots\dots\dots 6.3$$

(when V = Velocity, t = temperature, A and K are constants for the reaction in question.) From this it will be seen that the logarithm of reaction velocity is proportional to temperature.

This can also be written in the form

$$V_{(t+10)} = V_t Q_{10} \dots\dots\dots\dots\dots\dots\dots\dots\dots\dots\dots\dots\dots\dots\dots\dots\dots 6.4$$

in which the subsequent V_t = reaction velocity at a lower temperature V_t, $V_{(t+10)}$ is the velocity at a higher temperature 10°C above V_t, Q_{10} is the temperature coefficient. Normally, reactions proceed at about twice the rate when subjected to a temperature increase of 10°C. (For a detailed discussion of these laws see Andrewartha and Birch (1954) and Wigglesworth (1939 and later editions).) However, even at enzyme levels of complexity, departures from a simple $Q_{10} = 2$ relationship occur (see for instance Baldwin, 1948). Since the temperature range over which life is possible is, in any case, quite restricted, extensive conformity with the simple relationships expressed by the Q_{10} formula is not to be expected.

Basically, the use of the Q_{10} formula involves the hypothesis of an exponential increase of metabolic rate with temperature. This is not the only possible relationship, and, in fact, Krogh (1914) long ago suggested an alternative law which is based on a power series (see Jørgensen, 1916; Nielsen and Evans, 1960). In practice a considerable number of those who have worked with invertebrate animals have found that metabolic activity conforms more closely to Krogh's power law than that of the exponential law over a wide range of temperatures. This relationship exists, of course, only until the adverse affects of high temperature begin to be felt and the metabolic rate starts to decline. Examples are given by Nielsen and Evans (1960) and by Webb (1968).

Consistent results in accordance with such relationships depend, however, on measurements being made under reasonably realistic temperature conditions in such a way as to avoid the effects of acclimatization. When these conditions are not observed, and especially when the temperature changes are rapid, very much more extreme effects on the metabolic rate may be found. Berthet (1964), for instance, found that metabolic rate increased five times or more with the temperature rise of 10°C when oribatid mites were transferred between respirometers at 5°, 10°, 15° and 20°C within a few hours. Grainger (1956, 1958) detected oscillatory swings in the metabolic rate following sudden changes in temperature.

A useful analysis of short term changes in metabolic activity is due Newell (1966) who worked with a wide range of animals (Skate, *Actinia, Mytilus,*

Helix, and Locust). He found that there is a basic metabolism, reflected in that of the mitochondria of these animals, with a Q_{10} of only about 1.2 to 1.3. Superimposed on this, however, was a metabolic activity which persists for short periods only but has a much higher Q_{10} of about 1·85. This higher rate appears to be involved in behavioural response to rapid environmental change.

In general, the ecologist is not concerned with this extreme effect of environmental condition if only because these are usually avoided by animals as a result of their behaviour. Metabolic measurements are only of interest when they relate to the temperature ranges and rate of change which would be encountered in the natural habitat of the organisms at the time of year and of the life cycle which is under study.

Some controversy has been aroused by the question as to whether the metabolic activity of animals in an environment of fluctuating temperature exhibits respiratory rates which correspond to the arithmetical mean of the temperature or not. At least four possibilities could be envisaged: that the metabolism is that which would be expected from the arithmetical means, that which would be predictable from the geometric mean, that which would be predicted on a Q_{10} law and that which would be predicted from a power law (Krogh's law) or, finally, that the metabolism would be enhanced or suppressed by fluctuations approaching those normally experienced. No truly critical tests to discriminate between these possibilities have yet been devised. This is partly due, no doubt, to the non-availability of suitable equipment. Most results in this field (e.g. Butler, 1966) indicates that there is no significant departure from the metabolism to be expected from the mean temperature value. However, Messenger (1964) found that, as regards rate of development, an aphid and its braconid wasp parasite responded differentially to the change from constant to fluctuating conditions. This appears to have resulted in a relatively higher metabolism by the wasp in the latter circumstances.

Thus, not only do temperature/metabolism relationships certainly vary from species to species, but even between different life stages of the same species: O'Hara (1968), for instance, found in the sunfish that as the animal became older, the effect of temperature on the metabolic rate becomes more pronounced. It follows, once again that precise prediction of metabolic activity on the single species level demands all the resources of a physiological enquiry and that when cruder data only are available for ecological purposes it is essential to remember their limitations.

The effects of physical factors other than temperature on metabolism have been very little investigated except for studies on domestic animals. In the latter field, the separate effects of solar radiation, air movement and humidity have been examined especially in so far as they influence the effects of heat stress (see, for example, Findlay, 1950).

As already mentioned these other factors are often held at arbitrary or at even extreme values in respirometers and their influence is largely ignored. The effect of carbon dioxide on respiratory activities is one example. In the flea the addition of one per cent carbon dioxide to the air respired has the effect of increasing the period during which the spiracles are open by 50% and 2% carbon dioxide of keeping them permanently open (Wigglesworth, 1935).

Most subterranean arthropods live in an environment in which one per cent carbon dioxide is quite a normal concentration, but practically all measurements are made in Warburg type of respirometers in which the carbon dioxide level is maintained very close to zero. The effect of even half a per cent carbon dioxide on certain soil fungi in culture is known to be very great (Burges and Fenton, 1953). By replacing alkali with a carbon dioxide buffer, carbon dioxide levels of this magnitude were shown to halve the metabolic activity on similar fungi when grown in a semi-artificial soil (Macfadyen, in prep.).

Low humidity is another factor known to adversely affect the lives of many invertebrates in particular. The use of potassium hydroxide at 4% results in a relative humidity of 90% and anything as strong or stronger than this is almost certain to be harmful to most temperate invertebrates. A precise analysis of this factor is still apparently to be carried out.

It is clear, therefore, that the direct transposition of data from many physiological studies to ecological situations should be avoided and that the effects of many factors have been entirely overlooked. There is certainly an urgent need for further investigation of the reasons for the high variability of results obtained from respirometric work and there is some reason to hope that this variability can be reduced by a more precise analysis. Therefore it is essential that the conditions obtaining in respirometers should be recorded and that they should be related as far as possible to those that are likely to obtain in the normal environment until experiments can be conducted under more natural conditions.

6.2.5   Synthesis of laboratory metabolism data

In order that laboratory metabolism data should be of use to the ecologist for the study of energy flow in field populations it is strictly necessary that determinations of respiration should be made covering a sufficiently wide range of conditions of the kind discussed above. This has hardly been achieved as yet but some examples from the literature will show how far we have progressed and how much more remains to be done. The work of Klekowski *et al.* (1967) on *Tribolium* mentioned above (6.2.3) covers a full range of life stages and both sexes for an artificial population maintained at one set of physical environmental conditions and including a constant temperature, superabundant food and no mortality. In the case of this animal, which inhabits stored grain, there is no regular seasonal pattern of climate and the data obtained can be applied realistically to an expanding population which is not suffering mortality.

More usually, however, animals are subject to the seasonal variations of climate and here Healey's (1965) study of *Onychiurus procampatus* can be taken as a useful example. The insects were classified by size groups and the metabolism/temperature relationships were determined for each size group at intervals throughout the year. When related to the field data of population dynamics in the way to be discussed in section 6.4.3, this permits an estimate of field population metabolism.

An example of a study with four species of small mammals, which allows for life cycle stages and environmental temperature changes is the work of Górecki and Grodziński (1968). In this study laboratory determinations were made of the average daily metabolic rate (ADMR) and of the extra metabolism required for thermo-regulation and reproductive activities. The ADMR was related to body size by a regression function and the thermo-regulatory metabolism was derived from a similar equation making allowance for mutual warming behaviour of huddling in the nest, for the hours spent outside the nest and for ambient temperature. Separate determinations of metabolic costs of pregnancy and lactation were also made and incorporated in the final computation. In these examples the influence of physical life cycle factors have been adequately allowed for with the exception of conditions discussed at the end of the previous section. However, in all such work so far, lack of social interaction between individuals of the same species population have been assumed and the effects of social interactions, crowding, food shortage, etc. have been ignored. For further relation to field conditions it is, of course, necessary to incorporate in the model to be studied the effects of interspecific interaction and especially interactions with food supply organisms and with species which derive food from the population under study. These are factors which can only be studied realistically in the field situation and the topic will be taken up again in section 6.4.3.

6.3 Measurement of respiration rate in field populations: direct methods

In order to assess energy flow through a field population it would, ideally, be preferable if the metabolic activity of each organism could be continuously recorded — or at least integrated — without, in any way, interfering with its normal activities and to continue such measurements throughout the animal's life. Needless to say this situation has never been achieved, but recent technical developments have in fact made possible a number of approaches to it.

Three main principles are involved: (a) firstly some activity which is proportional to or related to metabolism is converted into an electric signal which is then either recorded in a data logger attached to the animal or else sent by telemetry or radio link to a recorder at a receiving station. (b) Secondly, the rate of elimination of some substance from the animal's body is related to metabolic rate under controlled conditions: then animals are released in the field and, when later recovered, the rate of elimination in the intervening period is determined. Most usefully the substance eliminated contains a radio-isotope, in which case standard nucleonic methods can be employed. (c) Thirdly, in certain uncommon circumstances, where a dense population of a single species monopolizes a limited volume of a habitat, this combination of population plus habitat can be treated as though it were a discrete organism and the metabolic rate of the whole is determined by respirometric or calorimetric methods.

None of these techniques is universally applicable but they have all the potential advantage of providing direct information on metabolic performance under field conditions, without the uncertainties and errors involved in extrapolating from laboratory experiments on individuals to whole populations in the field. On the other hand the greatest care is essential, especially in types (a) and (b) to ensure sufficient replication, so that results are not biassed by unusual animals or exceptional conditions. The principles and a few preliminary results of these approaches are detailed in sections 6.3.1 to 6.3.3.

6.3.1   Telemetry and recording of characteristics which are related to respiration rate

As indicated above, the principle behind studies of this kind (the use of which has been mainly confined to work with mammals) is to determine the relationship between a physiological quantity such as carbon dioxide content of expired air, breathing rate, heart rate on the one hand and total metabolic rate on the other. Then by means of an appropriate transducer electrical signals are recorded which can be related to the physiological quantity chosen. Recording might, theoretically, take place in a device carried by the animal or the signals can be transmitted by telemetry (usually using radio waves) and recorded at a stationary receiver. At the present time neither transmitters nor recorders (with their attendant batteries) are available for use with any organism smaller than the starlings which were studied by Haahn (1965) who worked with equipment weighing 24 g. However, newer electronic devices such as the tunnel diode (Ko and Thompson, 1963) offer the promise that telemetry from small mammals and possibly even large invertebrates will one day be feasible. With the advent of micro-miniature integrated circuits, the most severe weight limitations have been transferred from the electronic apparatus to the power supplies. This difficulty is being met by deriving power from heat gradients, mechanical movement or the interception of radiant energy. (Ko, 1965.) It is also helpful to limit the operation of the transmission to short intermittent periods which take place at regular intervals or in response to an interrogation signal from the monitoring station.

All the methods used so far have imposed restrictions on the animals' freedom of movement, such as those due to limited range of the radio transmitter, weight of the apparatus and batteries and inconvenience caused by the presence of the transducer.

As far as we are aware the use of simple light-weight integrators, carried by the animal, such as the Curtis meter (see Tanner *et al.*, 1963) does not seem to have been tried despite their low weight and low current demands.

Telemetry has been widely used for determining the spatial positions of animals and from such data an indication of locomotory activity can be obtained; examples and further references are cited in papers by Southern, Craighead and Craighead, Marshall, Cochran *et al.*, Siniff and Tester, who contributed to a special number of Bio-Science (see bibliography under Adams, 1965) and in a new book by Mackay (1968).

More fundamental problems which do not appear to have been fully solved are firstly the direct measurement of physiologically relevant parameters and secondly, the overcoming of the difficulty that quantitative errors are introduced both by the recording/transmitting methods and by non-linear relationships between the measured physiological parameter and the metabolic rate. It seems unlikely that such relationships will be simple and of the parameters mentioned above, perhaps carbon dioxide content of the breath measured by a catharometer (as employed in gas chromatography) is likely to be the quantity most easily related to true metabolic activity.

6.3.2 Measurement of elimination rates
(including the biological half-life of isotopes)

If it can be shown in the laboratory that the rate of elimination of a substance from an animal's body bears a predictable relationship to its metabolic rate, the possibility arises that, by measuring the content of the substance on two successive occasions, the metabolic activity during the intervening period can be estimated. This is true regardless of whether the animal was in captivity or was free in its normal environment.

In theory, the levels of any slowly eliminated foreign substance could be measured in, for example, the blood of a mammal but the only practical instances of the above principle known to us involve the use of radioactive isotopes. These have the great advantage that the total body concentration can be repeatedly determined from outside the animal's body without harming it.

Let us consider first a radioactive substance by itself and without relation to metabolic measurement. The radioactivity of any isotope decays in a predictable exponential manner such that, if the count rate or any other measure of activity is N_0 at $t = t_0$ (the beginning of a given time period) and is N_t at time t (the end of the same time period) and if λ is the decay constant, then

$$\frac{dN}{dt} = -\lambda N \quad \dotfill \quad 6.5$$

and

$$N_t = N_0 e^{-\lambda/t} \quad \dotfill \quad 6.6$$

The logarithms of a succession of count rate readings, when plotted against time, produce a straight line graph (Fig. 6.8). It is usual to express the count

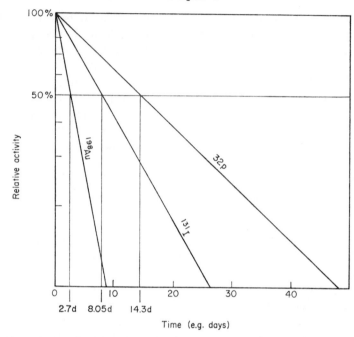

Figure 6.8. Radioactive decay of single isotopes. Abscissa=time. Ordinate=any measure of radioactivity, expressed as Nt/No and plotted logarithmically. Half life points on abscissa.

rate as percentages or decimals of the initial rate at $t = t_0$ and to plot the decimals of the original data on the ordinate of semi-logarithmic paper. When N falls to the value $N_0/2$ it follows that $e^{-\lambda/t} = \frac{1}{2}$.

This can be written

$$t_{\frac{1}{2}} = \log_e 2/\lambda = 0.693\ \lambda \dotfill 6.7$$

$t_{\frac{1}{2}} - t_0$ is called the 'half-life' of the isotope and the value $t_{\frac{1}{2}}$ is called the half-life time.

The reciprocal of λ is called the turnover rate $= k$. Since

$$k = \frac{1}{\lambda} \text{ and } t_{\frac{1}{2}} = \frac{0.693}{k}, \text{ it follows that}$$

$$k = \frac{0.693}{t_{\frac{1}{2}}} \dotfill 6.8$$

The physical half-lifes of isotopes vary from microseconds to millions of years. Some commonly encountered values are as follows:

Isotope	Half-Life
^{134}Cs	2·3 years
^{14}C	5,720 years
^{128}I	24·99 minutes
^{59}Fe	45·1 days
^{32}P	14·2 days
^{42}K	12·44 hours
^{86}Rb	19·5 days
^{46}Sc	85 days
^{87}Sr	28 hours
^{69}Zn	57 minutes

It follows from the exponential function of the decay rate of an isotope that after two half-lives the activity will have fallen to $N_0/4$, after three half-lives to $N_0/8$ and after m half-lives to $N_0/2^m$.

In order to determine the half-life of an unknown radioactive material it is, of course, only necessary to plot the successive values on semi-logarithmic paper and to interpolate the 50% value.

Where more than one isotope is present, it is usually possible to distinguish a faster and a slower component in the decay curve. In this case the slower rate curve is extrapolated to zero time first (Fig. 6.9) and its half-life determined. The activity attributed to that isotope is then subtracted from each of the initial readings, leaving a set of values which can then be plotted to determine the half-life of the isotope which had the faster decay rate.

Turning now to an isotope which has been assimilated by an organism and which is being eliminated at a rate proportional to its metabolic rate, a similar isotope elimination curve can be drawn and half-life determination made.

Frequently the curve due to biological elimination will be so steep in relation to the physical half-life that the latter will be but a small component in the overall rate of decay. In such cases the biological half-life is virtually the same as the quantity measured from the curve. Where an isotope is used which has a fairly short physical half-life it may be necessary to determine the biological half-life by the difference between the two logarithmic rates

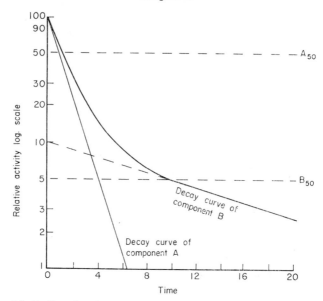

Figure 6.9. Radioactive decay of mixed isotopes. Abscissa=time. Ordinate=
logarithmic plot of Nt/No. To illustrate the method of extrapolating the lesser slope
to zero from isotope B and deriving the slope for isotope A by subtraction. A_{50} and
B_{50} denote the half life values for A and B resp.

in exactly the same way as the separation of physical half-lives in mixed
isotopes already discussed.

Earlier attempts to use this method such as that of Odum and Golley (1963)
who employed [69]Zn, showed that the decay rates could not be represented
on a logarithmic plot because radioactive zinc was taken up and released
differentially by different parts of the animal's body.

This kind of difficulty has led to some loss of confidence in such methods
until recently Reichle (1967) and Williams and Reichle (1968) reported a
variety of new approaches. In the latter case the herbivorous beetle *Chrysochus
auratus*, at least, revealed no evidence of the existence of such compartments
when [86]Rh is used as the isotope. In this case a very thorough study, involving
laboratory checks and tests on animals released in the field satisfied the
authors that the isotope elimination method was reliable.

The effective biological half-lives of the isotopes were first measured in
the laboratory using animals which were confined at 20°C and which were

fed contaminated leaves for some days until equilibrium nucleide burden had been reached. They were then removed to uncontaminated leaves. The biological turnover rate k was determined from successive counts of radioactivity using the formula

$$k = \frac{0 \cdot 693}{t_{\frac{1}{2}}}.$$

It was found that ^{32}P was retained for three or four times longer than ^{86}Rb there being also a partition effect and a difference between the sexes in the case of the radioactive phosphorus.

Beetles were then confined in cages in the field on plants which had been injected with about 200 μc of isotope. It was shown that the isotope content did not decline during the experiments. The beetles were periodically placed in the counter apparatus in gelatine capsules, a regression for absorption of β emission in relation to weight having been determined in a separate experiment in the case of [32]P.

Under these equilibrium conditions it was possible to obtain estimates of foliage consumption and assimilation of isotopes using the equation

$$C_I = \frac{kQ_eM}{a} \qquad \dots\dots\dots\dots\dots\dots\dots\dots\dots\dots\dots\dots\dots\dots\dots\dots\dots\dots\dots \quad 6.9$$

when:

C_I = isotope consumption
k = turnover rate
Q_e = equilibrium quantity
M = mass of beetle in mg dry wt
a = coefficient of assimilation of isotope

The estimates of foliage consumption were compared with normal gravimetric determinations. It was shown that the two sets of estimates did not differ significantly but that the isotope estimates were subject to smaller errors.

Although such techniques have only recently been developed and it is perhaps true to say that they have only been really satisfactory in the case of the one study reported there seems to be no doubt that this is potentially the best method available to us. Animals, once they have been fed or injected with isotope are free to move throughout their normal habitat in which they can live for an indefinite period encountering normal excursions of environmental variables and exhibiting normal rhythms of activity. After a desired interval at least a proportion of them can be traced and recaptured due to the radiation which they emit. Their isotope content is then detected and the animal can be released once more for further experimental periods and measurements.

A more sophisticated isotope technique is the $D_2{}^{18}O$ method in which the stable isotopes of hydrogen and oxygen are incorporated in water which is fed to the animal. Since the oxygen is eliminated both in water and in carbon dioxide, whilst the hydrogen is lost in water only, the turnover rate of the former is greater than of the latter and the difference in turnover rates is proportional to the carbon dioxide produced (see Golly, 1967; Lifson, Gordon and McClintock, 1955). The method involves the use of a mass spectrometer (expensive) and has not yet been fully tested, especially in the field. Preliminary work with migrating pigeons by Le Fèbre (1964) is, however, very promising.

6.3.3 Direct calorimetry in the field

This is a further technique which, although not yet widely practiced, illustrates an avenue of approach and offers the promise of avoiding the compounded errors of laboratory experiment and extrapolation in the field. Certain organisms have highly localized distributions and spend much of their lives closely clustered together either as a result of their exploitation of a single concentrated food source or as part of their social behaviour.

Examples of the first are insects which consume stored products, carcases, or mammalian dung pat species. Social insects, and man (when he is attending social functions) are instances of the latter. In theory the metabolic heat generated in such situations can be measured and it represents the metabolic activity of the population concerned under the current conditions. Two types of problem reduce the practicability of this approach; firstly, there are doubts about the extent to which the population is a single species and about the extent of the region which is subject to calorimetry. Secondly, there is the difficulty that individual organisms may spend part of their time away from the area of concentration and that the period they spend there may be atypical in terms of activity and energy budget.

The calorimetric principles, on the other hand, are not as difficult as might at first appear. For example the calorific output from a cinema or concert hall containing a thousand human beings can be fairly easily measured if the temperature rise in all the air flows leaving the building is multiplied by the specific heat of the air and its mass. The most important further corrections which must be applied involve firstly determination of the thermal capacity of the building (best measured empirically by liberating a known amount of heat energy, perhaps from electric heaters) and observing the resultant temperature rise. Secondly, allowance for changes in the humidity content of the air must be made because much heat is absorbed when water is vaporized.

It should be noted that by relating temperature rises to several different levels of heating and provided time is allowed for equilibration, it is not necessary to evacuate the people from the building. This is important in the case of the experiments which follow.

Although the temperature rise associated with insect infestations of stored products has been noted and measured, it does not appear to have been used to determine metabolic rates per individual (e.g. Denmead and Bailey, 1966). In this case the most serious additional problem would be the amount of extra heat liberated by micro-organisms in the medium. This, however, can be readily measured if the insects are removed from controlled samples (e.g. by sieving) provided allowance is made for effects of agitation of the substrate and resultant stimulation of microbial metabolism.

A preliminary attempt to use this approach in a field population of *Formica rufa* has also been reported (Macfadyen, 1967).

Some weeks before measurements are to be taken, heating wires, capable of dissipating about 20 watts from an automobile accumulator, are buried in the nest. Also buried are a number of resistance thermometers. The daily cycles of temperature in the nest are then measured over a week or more and compared with temperatures at a series of depths in the ground. During this period amounts of electrical power are also liberated in the heaters so as to determine the effect of the thermal capacity of the nest and any reactions of the ants to high temperature conditions. The results of this experiment were quite reasonable when compared with estimates based on laboratory respiration measurements and population counts.

This situation is further complicated by (a) the possibility that the ants will ventilate their nest under warm conditions (in practice this was met by the measurements referred to and by confining observations to cooler weather), (b) the fact that many ants spend much of their time outside the nest (this involves counting the moving ants or restricting observations to times when they stay in the nest).

6.4   Indirect calculation of field energy flow from the combination of field and laboratory data

6.4.1   Problems of extrapolation from field to laboratory

In the previous sections, repeated reference has inevitably been made to the complications associated with the use of laboratory data on metabolism in order to extrapolate populations under field conditions. These are fundamentally of two kinds. There are differences involved in simulating in the laboratory the conditions in the field environment, partly due to technical demands of respirometers and colorimeters and even more due to the very great difficulties associated with measuring the true climatic and other conditions actually experienced by a free living organism. Secondly, there are difficulties associated with reconstructing, not only the field population structure (in terms of age, sex, mortality of different age classes, etc.) but also its energy budget experience in terms of food consumption, digestive efficiency and so on.

Individually, none of these problems is insuperable. Some courageous attempts have already been made, whilst further combined studies are being undertaken especially in the context of the International Biological Programme, to piece together the many items of information required to construct the whole picture. However, the sheer bulk of information required and the cost in money and manpower which its aquisition demands has led to the realization that carefully directed projects, standardization of compatible data, the use of systems analysis, of critical path analysis and of other sophisticated computable programmes will be required if the analysis of energy flow in the more complicated ecosystems is to be made possible.

6.4.2   The effect of environmental factors on the respiration rate

The general effect of environmental factors on laboratory determinations of metabolic rate has been treated in section 6.2.4. There are, however, a number of special problems involved in extending such knowledge to field conditions. These are especially associated with the extreme variability of physical conditions in many natural environments both in space and in time and also with the difficulty of ascertaining the true relationship between the position, in relation to such distributions, of an 'average' individual and, even further, the full range of individuals. For example temperature profiles within a few centimetres of the surface of soil even in temperate countries, can range over 20°C or more. The daily rhythm involves a peak temperature at the surface soon after mid-day. However, even three centimetres below this the daily maximum may well occur in the middle of the night. Many small invertebrates are capable of migrating over this depth and almost nothing is known of the patterns of vertical distribution of most species in such situations. Until the true diurnal thermal experience of such creatures in nature is known, there is little hope of extending to the field precise laboratory determinations of the effect of temperature on metabolism. It is a most discomforting thought, therefore, that such laboratory experiments have indeed revealed the marked influence of temperature on metabolism which was discussed in section 6.2.4.

A further difficulty is the problem of obtaining realistic microclimate determinations under the actual field conditions encountered by the invertebrates. The spatial distribution of temperature is very complicated. Soil, for instance, does not, in nature, present an easily identified horizontal reference plane and the only hope of avoiding gross errors appears to be to make very large numbers of measurements. If such spatial diversification is to be achieved in the measurements and if we are to account for the rapid changes which occur in time, only two approaches seem to be possible. Either a very costly programme, involving numerous sensors and data logging which is compatible with computer analysis must be undertaken; or we should use large numbers of simple integrating devices which can be replicated cheaply (Macfadyen, 1968). Although in the end the latter may be more costly in manpower it may sometimes prove the only possible approach and, in view of the uncertain biological basis of most microclimatic measurements, it appears to be fully justified in many cases.

In the case of larger animals the problem is not so great. As long ago as 1940 Krogh described a micro-thermo-hydrograph for human use which was based on a converted wrist-watch and was used to explore the climate of different parts of the human body especially in relation to the influence of clothing. This contained not only sensors for temperature (a bimetal) and for humidity (a hair) but also the complete recorder. The results were read under a microscope. Modern technology should make it possible to reduce such a device to a size which might be carried by a small mammal, perhaps incorporating telemetry (see 6.3.1), but the influence of temperatures within the normal range is usually less extreme in homoitherms and such devices have not yet been developed for use with poikilotherms.

6.4.3 Synthesis of population and respiration-rate data in order to estimate total field population metabolism

From the preceding sections it will be seen that the annual total of energy liberated by a field population depends on:

the density of the population;
the composition of the population in terms of age, sex and other demographic categories;
the physical conditions actually experienced by the individual animals;
the composition and quality of their food supplies.

All these parameters vary greatly both in space and in time. It is necessary, therefore, to define very precisely the area occupied by the population and to ensure that a sufficient time span is covered. Even an entire year or generation length may not, in many animals suffice to provide experience of a characteristic range of population density and, with regard to spatial distribution there may be persistent variations in density (not obvious to the investigator) in addition to population movements which result in both short and long term changes in distribution patterns.

Such a list of difficulties might lead one to conclude that no worthwhile field metabolism studies are possible. However, increasing numbers of ecologists have, in fact, completed field studies on populations which, despite their admitted inaccuracies have contributed greatly to our understanding of ecosystems. Examples, which have already been mentioned, from terrestrial organisms include the work of Edgar (1968), Healey (1965, 1967), Phillipson (1962, 1963, 1967), Webb (1968) and Wiegert (1965). Among studies of aquatic organisms those by Mann (1964) on freshwater fish and by Hughes (1968) on an estuarine bivalve mollusc deserve special attention.

In all such investigations to date a large number of simplifying assumptions have been made as has been discussed in section 6.0. It follows that the accuracy of the final estimates of field population metabolism must be low and the cumulative effect of errors uncertain. In the study of a population of a soil invertebrate, for example, errors will arise from such sources as:

the non-random distribution of the population and sampling errors;
interpolation of population estimates between monthly (or even weekly) census occasions;

variability in the regression of metabolic activity on age or size categories; extrapolation from laboratory conditions to field conditions when estimating metabolic and production parameters;
uncertainties and errors in determining the precise physical environment experienced by the animals;
ignorance of the food supplies and their nutrient status.

The cumulative effects of errors from all these sources may well result in overall estimates being two or three times too high or too low. But in the context of whole ecosystem studies even errors of this magnitude may not render the results valueless.

Firstly the information is largely required for comparative purposes: comparisons between competing species and between different food chains. Secondly the differences between productivity parameters in successive trophic levels may greatly exceed this order of magnitude: by a factor of ten or more.

Thirdly there is an overall balance in the energy budget for a whole community such that the intake of solar energy plus gains from other communities is equal to the losses through respiration and outward transport. This budget provides an overall check on the individual items within it so that if comparative, as opposed to absolute, magnitudes are known these can be scaled up or down as evidence from other parts of a community becomes available. By such comparisons and by judicious reinvestigation of obviously anomalous results insight is already being gained into the general distribution of energy flow within whole ecosystems and it is becoming possible to compare the patterns of different systems one with another. This is discussed in section 7.

7

The Place of Secondary Producers
in the Ecosystem

7.1 The trophic level concept and its imperfections

The concept of the Trophic level has proved most fruitful in promoting and systematising ecological ideas; it has encouraged ecologists to look beyond the role and functioning of single species to those of whole communities. But there can be doubt that, as applied to most ecosystems it is a gross over-simplification and the extent to which its uncritical adoption leads to distortion of our understanding has hardly yet been assessed.

Earlier food-chain studies were largely based on generalisations about the type of food consumed by particular species or frequently by whole groups. Later more detailed work has frequently shown that almost no taxonomic group and remarkably few species restrict their diets at all narrowly. Among small mammals it has been generally assumed that *Apodemus flavicollis*, for instance, is a herbivore feeding on roots and seeds; work by Polish workers shows that in fact the diet may easily include insects and other animal food. A few examples among invertebrates may also be given:

(a)   The Opiliones were generally thought of as scavengers of dead animals until Phillipson (1960) and colleagues showed that they were mainly carnivorous.

(b)   The nematodes in soil were thought to feed on living and rotting plant matter until Neilsen (1949) showed that they include a high proportion of feeders on algae, bacteria, protozoa and on other nematodes.

(c)   The chilopods such as *Lithobius* species were always regarded as strict carnivores until Blower (1968) showed that *L. forficatus* can eat at least equal quantities of plant materials although *L. variegatus* appears to be more strictly carnivorous.

(d)   A further example which involves the reversal of normal preconceptions not only between Trophic levels but also between whole sections of an ecosystem is the demonstration by Gliwicz (see 5.4.3) that species of Rotifer usually thought of as herbivores grazing on planktonic algae, may in fact derive most of their food from bacteria. By cropping members of the decomposer food web they thus transfer energy from it to the 'grazing food chain' and to the predators thereon.

(e) The Collembola are generally thought of as feeders on soil microorganisms; it now seems clear that some species of *Onychiurus* can attack higher plants and cause economic damage (Edwards, 1962), that *Friesia* can feed on rotifers, protura and tardigrades, (Cassagnau 1961), that *Anurida* can feed on decaying animal flesh (Miles, 1947) and there is an old record by Macnamara of one species of *Isotoma* which is predatory on other Collembola. The whole subject has recently been reviewed by Christiansen (1964).

It is well known of course that endopterygote insects may feed quite differently as larvae and as adults: for instance many blood sucking Diptera have herbivorous larvae whilst many dung flies feed on nectar as adults and on dung as larvae. However, in addition, the relative proportions of different foods in the diet of animals vary from one season to another and in different stages in the life cycle. Examples are numerous, especially among birds (Hartley, 1953; Lack, 1968) and small mammals (Crowcroft, 1957) and freshwater fish (Horton, 1961; Hartley, 1948; Elliott, 1967). The last paper shows that in the case of trout not only do the organisms eaten change with the season but there is also a consistent pattern of feeding on 'drift' animals in the summer and on bottom living organisms in the winter.

Further complications to the simple food chain concept are caused by the mobility of animals. It has frequently been remarked, for instance, that there appear to be an excessive number of carnivores in certain habitats and insufficient food organisms to supply them. In part this may be because the prey breed more rapidly and are continuously being cropped. The result of this is that the standing crop of prey species gives a false impression of their production rate. This is especially true in the case of carnivorous fish feeding on invertebrates (Allen, 1951; Horton, 1961) and probably applies to groups like the mesostigmatic mites and spiders which have generation times of a year or more in contrast to many of their food animals which have several generations in a year. However, a further major factor is the movement of animals between habitats. Much of the food of litter living carnivores consists of diptera, caterpillars, aphids and other forms whose nourishment was derived from completely different habitats. For instance the spiders living in meadows studied by Kajak (1967) and colleagues were found to feed largely on mosquitoes which originated from emergent and aquatic ecosystems in quite different areas.

It follows from the above considerations that generalizations about feeding relationships can lead to serious errors, both quantitative and qualitative unless due account is taken of the mobility of animals between systems, and the changes of diet with life stage and season. Further inaccuracy often arises when generalizations about the feeding behaviour of one species are extended to others even when they are closely related from a taxonomic point of view.

7.2 Secondary production in relation to primary production

Secondary production in natural ecosystems depends in the first place on net primary productivity. It has been somewhat of a surprise (and a disappointment) to find that in tropical climates the latter do not appear to increase in proportion to increased sunlight. The diagrams in Fig. 7.1 (based on Müller and Nielsen, 1965), and on Møller *et al.* (1954a, 1954b), show that, despite a tenfold increase in solar energy reaching the earth's surface in

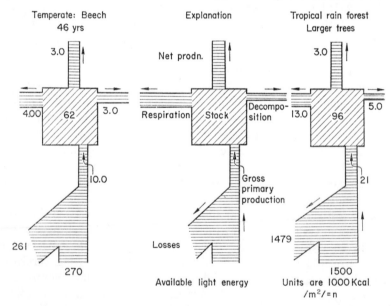

Figure 7.1. Partitioning of primary production in tropical and temperate forests. Logarithmic scale diagrams permit comparison between energy flows through the primary producers (forest trees) and their relative biomass. (Scale as in Figure 7.2.)

tropical forests the amount of energy available to secondary producers has hardly increased at all. This appears to be largely due to increased respiration by tropical plants themselves. It might be suggested, too, that this situation results from higher temperatures and perhaps also from the need for special adaptations such as increased trunk size (non-photosynthetic) demanded by greater competition between the trees. Perhaps, too, man has more to learn about the exploitation of tropical crops, for it is clear that many attempts to introduce cultural practices evolved in temperate climates have been very ill-suited to uncritical application in the tropics. A similar relationship exists between tropical and temperate grasslands and between tropical and temperate planktonic communities. Despite higher photosynthetic rates the tropical plant uses up so much more energy for its own metabolism that there is little gain in the amount available to secondary producers.

On the other hand the really striking differences between the pattern of exploitation of primary production do occur when comparisons are made between systems which are based on different major plant types. (Fig. 7.2

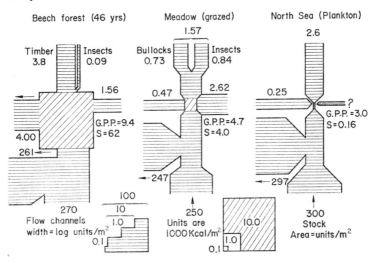

Figure 7.2. A comparison between the energy flow pattern in three types of temperate ecosystem. (Scheme as in Figure 7.1.)

based on Macfadyen, 1963b, 1964.) The large plants, which lock up large amounts of energy in their tissues require a higher proportion thereof for their own metabolic purposes. The microscopic plants such as algae carry out almost as much photosynthesis with a much smaller biomass; they respire less themselves and make more available to the herbivores presumably because a lower proportion is respired, because these simple plants are usually more palatable and also because their rate of turnover is much higher. In the case of grasslands an intermediate situation appears to obtain; an intermediate size of standing crop is fairly well defended against herbivores but it makes more material available to secondary levels. The result is the production of a large amount of litter and the support of a decomposer trophic group which is much more important than the herbivores.

At first sight, then, it would appear that traditional exploitation of grass-feeding cattle may be approaching the limits of what is biologically possible. But if we could derive our animal food from tree leaves or better still from consumers of microscopic plants, herbivore production/consumption efficiency might well be much higher. Finally, we must remember that the simple food chain concept has to some extent misled us: that many links do in fact bridge over from one chain to another. If the rotifers can derive nourishment from bacteria and supply it via Crustacea to fish (and many copepods, too, are now known to feed at least partly on bacteria) then we can certainly expect transfer to the herbivore-carnivore chains from the grassland decomposer system.

In a classic series of experiments in which *Daphnia* were artificially 'cropped' and the maximum sustainable yield was measured, Slobodkin (1954, 1959) showed that the peak efficiency of energy transfer from the algal food of the *Daphnia* to the crop was of the order of 15%. Further experiments on other species and theoretical considerations convinced him that this figure applies quite generally through the animal kingdom (1960).

In agricultural practice, in which animals such as the pig and cow have long been selected to maximise secondary production and production/consumption efficiency, figures about twice as high as this have been achieved (Duckham, 1963) but it must be remembered that such animals no longer have to forage for their food or defend themselves against predators and are thus able to divert energy into production which otherwise would probably be lost in maintaining structures not directly concerned with the production of flesh or in extra metabolic activity.

There remains the possibility that certain groups of herbivores may, within the limits suggested by Slobodkin, show a general trend towards higher or lower production/consumption ratios. Data are sparse and generlisation is difficult but it certainly appears that homoitherms, other than the domestic animals already mentioned, respire a higher proportion of their food consumption than do many invertebrates. This is clearly shown by figures given in table 7.1 derived from Wiegert and Evans (1967). The insects

TABLE 7.1. Population energy data from N. American Old Field Systems and African grasslands.

(All figures are in kcal/m².)

Animals	Location	Production	Consumption	P/C
Orthoptera	S. Carolina	4·00	76·9	0·05
	Michigan	0·51	3·71	0·14
	Salt Marsh	11·00	107·00	0·10
Plant hoppers	Salt Marsh	70·00	413·00	0·17
	Michigan	0·08	1·51	0·05
Other insects	S. Carolina	0·40	7·70	0·05
	Michigan	0·10	0·71	0·14
Harvester ant	S. Carolina	0·09	34·5	0·003*
Sparrows	S. Carolina	0·04	4·00	0·01
	Michigan	0·05	2·55	0·02
Old field mouse	S. Carolina	0·12	7·40	0·02
Deer mice	Michigan	0·01	1·08	0·01
Ground squirrels	Michigan	0·11	5·60	0·02
Ungulates	Tanganyika	4·00	273·30	0·01
Elephants	Tanganyika	0·34	71·60	0·05

* This figure is probably unreliable and has been challenged.

generally appear to be highly productive and use a relatively small part of their assimilated energy in respiration when compared with vertebrates. There is an important point to remember, however, when attempting to use published data on insect growth and metabolism: most of the figures apply to insects which have been kept under artificial conditions and subject to mortality only when fully grown. If a suitable predator were to arrange to protect an insect population until maturity he would be exploiting a very efficient system, but the vast majority of insect *populations* in nature have completely different properties and are subject to very heavy mortality especially in the youngest age groups. As a result, the youngest ages, which respire proportionately much faster than the older ones (see 6.2.3) contribute very little to total population production and the whole situation is far less favourable to a potential exploiter. Wiegart and Evans suggest that man should attempt to become just such a predator and should in this way make use of a potentially most productive source of high protein nourishment.

In general, then, the study of secondary production is still in its early stages and there must be many surprises yet to come. But it would appear that, whilst existing tropical terrestrial ecosystems seem to offer less hope for high levels of secondary production than either temperate, terrestrial or planktonic systems, in terms of the kind of organism which is exploited there is ample scope for innovation. In particular the microorganisms (both autotrophic and decomposing) and the invertebrates should receive attention as potential converters to high quality animal food.

7.3 The contribution of secondary producers to energy and nutrient flow through ecosystems

Quite apart from their significance as 'upgraders' of plant matter and detritus and as secondary producers, hetrotrophic organisms play a general role in the functioning of whole ecosystems without which, of course, such systems could not exist. This is because inorganic nutrients such as nitrogen and phosphorus and potash and various trace elements, which are incorporated in organic matter by plants are usually in short supply in soil and in ground water. They are only made available again in the faeces, excretions and corpses of hetrotrophic organisms.

The measurement of these effects is made very difficult because the greater the demand for nutrient by plants the shorter will be the period in which they exist free in solution and thus the lower the concentrations available for analysis. In fact, in certain nutrient-starved ecosystems such as those which develop in peat soils the entire circulation of nutrients appears to be confined within tussocks of plants such as *Eriophorum* (Goodman, 1963) and passes directly from old leaves to new tussocks, partly by withdrawal as the leaf dies and partly by active absorption through the surface of young leaves.

Any animal or other hetrotroph which consumes plant matter and excretes inorganic ions is contributing to the general circulation of nutrients and does so roughly in proportion to its respiratory metabolism; this is, in turn, contributing to the recirculation of carbon and the energy flow through the whole system. It is this interlinking of the passage of nutrients, carbon and energy through ecosystems which is the justification for using metabolic measurements as preliminary criteria of importance and of their contribution to the functional activity of the system as a whole: the way in which this can be done has already been demonstrated in part 6.

Appendix

Constants and conversions useful in calculations involving energy and biomass

A. Conversions between units

1 m   = 39·3701 inches
1 ha   = 2·4711 acres
1 kg   = 2·046 lbs
1 tonne = 0·9849 ton
1 Joule = 10^7Erg = 0·28.10^{-6}KWhr = 0·239 cal
1 KWhr = 3·6.10^{-6}Joule = 1·36 HPhr = 0·86.10^6 cal
1 HPhr = 2·65.10^6 Joule = 0·736 KWhr = 633.10^3 cal
1 cal   = 41·86.10^6Erg = 4·186 Joule = 1·163.10^{-6}KWhr = 1·58.10^{-6}HPhr = 0·00397 BThU
1 BThU = 1043 Joule = 0·000393 HPhr = 252 cal

B. Constants and useful quantities

The Solar constant (= the solar energy received at a plane normal to the sun's direction outside the earth's atmosphere) = 2·00 cal/cm²/min. Annual mean radiation at the earth's surface at 54°N latitude = 0·93 cal/cm²/min; of this a maximum of 14% is used in photosynthesis, after losses due to reflection and limited spectral response.

Density of Oxygen at N.T.P.*   = 1·429 g/l
            Oxygen at 20°C   = 1·331 g/l
            Carbon dioxide at N.T.P. = 1·977 g/l**
            Carbon dioxide at 20°C   = 1·842 g/l
            Air at N.T.P.   = 1·293 g/l
            Air at 20°C   = 1·205 g/l

Approximate basal metabolism of a mammal of body weight Wkg = $70W^{\frac{3}{4}}$ (kcal/day).

---

* N.T.P. normal temperature and pressure.
** 1.965 at low concentrations: see text under Respiratory quotient.

C. Composite quantities

(a) Mass per unit area

1 g/m^2 = 1 tonne/km^2 = 0.1 kg/ha = 0.1124 lb/acre

1 kg/ha = 10 g/m^2 = 1.124 lb/acre

(b) Energy release per unit area

(Assuming 4,800 cal are liberated in the respiration of 1 g of organic matter.)

1 g/m^2 = $4,800$ cal/m^2 = 480 kcal/ha

O_2 consumption of 1 g/m^2 = 252 cal/m^2 = 25.2 kcal/ha

CO_2 evolution of 1 g/m^2 = 289 cal/m^2 = 28.9 kcal/ha

1 S.N.U./ha = 100 kcal/m^2 (S.N.U. = Standard Nutrional Unit)

(c) Energy release per unit area and time

1 cal/cm^2/min = $14.4.10^6$ cal/m^2/day = $5.25.10^9$ cal/m^2/year

$\qquad = 52.5.10^3$ S.N.U./ha/year

1 S.N.U./ha/year = 10^6 kcal/ha/year = 10^5 cal/m^2/year

$\qquad = 274$ cal/m^2/day = $19.05.10^{-6}$ cal/cm^2/min.

D. Calorific equivalents and gaseous exchange associated with the combustion of common foodstuffs and organic compounds

In GENERAL. The energy liberated per litre of carbon dioxide produced by burning a carbon compound is $\dfrac{12}{22.4}$ = 0.5357 times the energy content of the substance per gram of carbon.

Thus if carbon content (as a decimal) = C

if heat of combustion per g substance = H kcal

then energy liberated per litre of carbon dioxide (E) = $\dfrac{0.5357H}{C}$

e.g. if H = 5 kcal/g, C = 50%, then E = $\dfrac{5}{0.5} \times 0.5357 = 5.357$ kcal/l.

Respiratory quotient, R.Q.

R.Q. = the ratio of mols CO_2 produced to mols O_2 consumed in respiration. In practice mols are equivalent to volumes (although CO_2 is not an ideal gas, at the low concentrations encountered by organisms, it is effectively so and the theoretical density of 1·965 obtains). The ratio may be calculated, using the percentage composition of the different elements, from the ratio of gram atoms of excess carbon to the total oxygen required in combustion. In carbohydrates the volumes of gas are equal and the ratio is unity. In the case of fats and proteins respectively the quotients are of the order of 0·71 and 0·80 respectively. When fat is being synthesised from carbohydrates within the body, RQ values above unity may be observed whilst synthesis of carbohydrates may depress the values. Thus short term observations of R.Q. are of little value.

E. Calorific and gaseous exchange of some common foods (in calories and g of gas per g of substance)

PURE SUBSTANCES	R.Q.	Calories	O_2	CO_2
Carbohydrates	1·0	3,700–4,200	1·59	2·21
Fat	0·71	9,500	2·90	2·84
Protein	0·80	3,900–4,150	1·22–1·29	1·32–1·40
FOODSTUFFS				
Approximate average	0·82	4,000	1·22	1·38
Cereals		3,600–4,300		
Root vegetables		3,400–3,800		
Leguminous vegetables		3,400–3,800		
Green vegetables		2,600–3,100		
Fruits		3,300–3,800		
Leaf litter		4,800		
Mammalian meats		6,400–7,400		
Poultry meats		5,900–7,000		
Fish meats		4,000–4,400		
Milk (cow's)		5,200		
Cheese		6,300		

F. Table of calorific contents and equivalents of carbohydrate, fat and protein.

Food Substances	R.Q.	Calories Liberated During					Oxidation of 1 mg Food Involves				Liberation of 1 calorie Involves			
		Combustion of 1 mg	Oxygen uptake of 1 cc	1 mg	Carbon dioxide production of 1 cc	1 mg	Oxygen uptake of cc	mg	Carbon dioxide production of cc	mg	Oxygen uptake of cc	mg	Carbon dioxide production of cc	mg
Carbohydrate solid	1·0	5·65	5·05* (4·60)	3·57	5·05	2·56	1·12	1·59	1·12	2·21	0·198	0·280	0·198	0·390
Fat (oils)	0·71	9·35	(4·40)	3·22	6·5	3·06	2·04	2·91	1·44	2·84	0·218	0·310	0·154	0·327
Protein { plant	0·79	4·15	4·6	3·22	5·83	2·95	0·90	1·29	0·71	1·40	0·218	0·310	0·171	0·339
Protein { animal		3·90					0·85	1·22	0·67	1·32				
Dry plant matter and approximate human diet	0·82	4·0	4·7	3·29†	5·7	2·88	0·85	1·22	0·70	1·38	0·212	0·304	0·175	0·347

Notes: Volumes of gases are at N.T.P.

calories are small or gramme calories

Density of Oxygen at N.T.P. is taken as 1·429 g per litre, of CO_2 as 1·977 g per litre

* Glycogen 5·14, Starch 5·06, Sucrose 5·08

† Ivlev's (1934) Oxycaloric equivalent is given as 3·38 cal per mg O_2

Note that the range of oxygen-uptake figures associated with the liberation of one calorie is about 5 per cent, that for the carbon dioxide is about 18 per cent.

References

ADAMS L. (1959). An analysis of a population of snowshoe hares in north-western Montana. *Ecol. Monogr.* **29**, 141–170.

ADAMS L. (1965). Progress in ecological telemetry. Special number containing twelve articles and extensive bibliography mentioned in the text. *BioScience* **15**, 83–157.

ADAMS L., O'REGAN W.G. & DUNAWAY D.J. (1962). Analysis of forage consumption by faecal examination. *J. Wildlife Mgmt.* **26**, 108–111.

ALLEE W.C., EMERSON A.E., PARK O., PARK T. & SCHMIDT K.P. (1955). *Principles of Animal Ecology*. Philadelphia and London. 837 pp.

ALLEN K.R. (1951). The Horokiwi Stream. *Bull. mar. Dep. N.Z. Fish.* No. **10**, 1–231.

ANDERSEN J. (1950). Harer og Frugttrager. *Dansk Jagttidende* **67**, 225–228.

ANDREWARTHA H.G. (1961) *Introduction to the study of Animal Populations*. Methuen.

ANDREWARTHA H.G. & BIRCH L.C. (1954). *The Distribution and Abundance of Animals*. Chicago. 782 pp.

ANDRZEJEWSKA L. (1967). Estimation of the effects of feeding of the sucking insect *Cicadella viridis* L. on plants. In: *Secondary Productivity of Terrestrial Ecosystems* (*Principes and Methods*), ed. K. Petrusewicz, Warszawa-Kraków. pp. 791–805.

ANDRZEJEWSKA L., BREYMEYER A., KAJAK A. & WÓJCIK Z. (1967). Experimental studies on trophic relationships of terrestrial invertebrates. In: *Secondary Productivity of Terrestrial Ecosystems* (*Principles and Methods*), ed. K. Petrusewicz, Warszawa-Kraków. pp. 477–495.

ANDRZEJEWSKI R. & JEZIERSKI W. (1966). Studies on the European Hare. XI. Estimation of population density and attempt to plan the yearly take of hares. *Acta theriol.* **11**, 433–448.

BALDWIN E. (1948). *Dynamic Aspects of Biochemistry*. Cambridge. 20–22 refer. (See also later editions.)

BALOGH J. (1958a). *Lebensgemeinschaften der Landtiere*. Berlin. 560 pp.

BALOGH J. (1958b). On some problems of production biology. *Acta zool. Sci. Hung.* **4**, 89–114.

BARCROFT J. (1908). Differential method of blood-gas analysis. *J. Physiol.* **37**, 12–24.

BERTALANFFY L. VON. (1957a). *Handbuch der Zoologie*. Berlin.

BERTALANFFY L. VON. (1957b). Quantitative laws in metabolism and growth. *Quart. Rev. Biol.* **32**, 217–231.

BERTHET P. (1963). Mesure de la consommation d'oxygène des Oribatides (Acariens) de la litière des Forets. In: *Soil Organisms*, ed. J. Doeksen & J. van der Drift. Amsterdam. pp. 18–31.

BERTHET P. (1964). L'activité des Oribatides d'une Chênaie. *Mem. Inst. Roy. Sci. Nat. Belg.* No. **152**, 1–152.

BERTHET P. (1967). The metabolic activity of oribatid mites (*Acarina*) in different forest floors. In: *Secondary Productivity of Terrestrial Ecosystems* (*Principles and Methods*), ed. K. Petrusewicz, Warszawa-Kraków. pp. 709–725.

164   *References*

BETTS M. (1956). Further experiments with an artificial nesting gape. *Brit. Birds* **49**, 213–215.
BLOWER J.G. (1969). The age structure of millipede populations in relation to activity and dispersion. In; *The Soil Ecosystem*. Systematics Association, London. Publication No. 8.
BOCOCK K.L. (1963). The digestion and assimilation of food by *Glomeris*. In: *Soil organisms*, ed. J. Doeksen & J. van der Drift, Amsterdam. pp. 85–91.
BÖRNEBUSCH C.H. (1930). The fauna of forest soil. *Det. forstl. Forsogsv.* **11**, 1–158.
BORUTZKY E.V. (1939). [Dynamics of *Chironomus plumosus* in the profundal of lake Beloie]. *Arb. Proc. Limnol. Sta. Kossino* **22**, 156–195, 196–218. (In Russian with English summary.)
BOUCHNER M. (1960). Aktivität und Nahrungsbedarf der Kohlmaeisen während der Brutzeit. *Probl. angew. Orn. Tagungsberichte* No. **30**, 35–44.
BOWMAN G.E. (1968). The measurement of carbon dioxide concentration in the atmosphere. In: *The Measurement of Environmental Factors in Terrestrial Ecology*, ed. R.M. Wadsworth, Blackwell, Oxford. pp. 131–139.
BRAY J.R. (1961). Measurement of leaf utilization as an index of minimum level of primary consumption. *Oikos* **12**, 71–74.
BREYMEYER A. (1967a). Correlations between dry weight of spiders and their length and fresh weight. *Bull. Acad. pol. Sci. Cl. II*, **15**, 263–265.
BREYMEYER A. (1967b). Preliminary data for estimating the biological production of wandering spiders. In: *Secondary Productivity of Terrestrial Ecosystems* (*Principles and Methods*), ed. K. Petrusewicz, Warszawa-Kraków. pp. 821–834.
BRISTOWE W.S. (1933). The spiders of Bear Island. *Norsk Ent. Tidskr.* **3**, 149–154.
BRODY S. (1945). *Bioenergetics and growth*. New York. 1023 pp.
BRZIN M., VETTBARN W.D., ROSENBERG P. & IVACHMANSON D. (1965). Cholinesterase activity per unit surface area of conducting membranes. *J. Cell. Biol.* **26**, 353–364.
BUCKNER C.H. (1967). The estimation of energy flow through the populations of birds. In: *Secondary Productivity of Terrestrial Ecosystems* (*Principles and Methods*), ed. K. Petrusewicz, Warszawa-Kraków. pp. 163–179.
BUJALSKA G., ANDRZEJEWSKI R. & PETRUSEWICZ K. (1968). Productivity investigation of an island population of *Clethrionomys glareolus* (Schreber, 1780). II. Natality. *Acta theriol.* **13**, 415–425.
BUJALSKA G. & GLIWICZ J. (1968). Productivity investigation of an island population of *Clethrionomys glareolus* (Schreber, 1780). III. Individual growth curve. *Acta theriol.* **13**, 427–433.
BURGES H. & FENTON E. (1953). The effect of carbon dioxide on the growth of certain soil fungi. *Trans. Brit. mycol. Soc.* **36**, 104–108.
BUTLER T. & BUTLER G.D. (1966). Development of the beet armyworm and its parasite *Chetonus texanus* in relation to temperature. *J. econ. Ent.* **59**, 1324–1327.
CALHOUN J.B. (1964). The social use of space. In: *Physiological Mammalogy*, ed. W.V. Mayer & R.G. van Gelder. New York. 187 pp.
CALVET E. & PRAT H. (1956). *Mircrocalorimétrie*. Masson, Paris. 396 pp.
CALVET E. & PRAT H. (1963). *Recent Progress in Microcalorimetry*. Pergammon.
CASSAGNAU P. (1961). *Les biocenoses des collemboles*. In: *Ecologie du Sol dans les Pyrenées centrales*. Hermann, Paris. 235 pp.

CHRISTIANSEN K. (1964). Bionomics of Collembola. *Ann. Rev. Ent.* **9**, 147–178.

CLARKE G.L. (1954). *Elements of Ecology.* London and New York. 534 pp.

CLOUDSLEY-THOMPSON J.L. (1951a). Studies in diurnal rhythms. 1. Rhythmic behaviour of millipedes. *J. exp. Biol.* **28**, 165–172.

CLOUDSLEY-THOMPSON J.L. (1951b). On the sensory responses to environmental stimuli and the sensory physiology of the millipedes (*Diplopoda*). *Proc. zool. Soc. Lond.* **121**, 253–275.

CLOUDSLEY-THOMPSON J.L. (1953). Diurnal rhythms in animals. *Science News* (Harmondsworth) **28**, 76–79.

COLE L.C. (1954). The population consequences of life history phenomena. *Quart. Rev. Biol.* **29**, 103–137.

COLEMAN D.C. & MACFADYEN A. (1966). The recolonisation of gamma-irradiated soil by small arthropods. *Oikos* **17**, 62–70.

COMITA G.W. & SCHINDLER D.W. (1963). Calorific values of microcrustacea. *Science* **140**, 1394–1396.

CONWAY E.J. (1950). *Microdiffusion Analysis and Volumetric Error.* (First published 1939, 2nd edn. 1947.) Crosby Lockwood, London. 357 pp.

COX G.W. (1961). The relation of energy requirements of tropical finches to distribution and migration. *Ecology* **42**, 253–265.

CRAGG J.B. (1961). Some aspects of the ecology of moorland soils. *J. Anim. Ecol.* **30**, 205–234.

CROSSLEY D.A. JR. (1963). Consumption of vegetation by insects. In: *Radioecology,* ed. V. Schultz & A.W. Klement, Jr. Reinhold, New York. pp. 427–430.

CROWCROFT P. (1957). *The life of the Shrew.* Rheinhardt, London. 166 pp.

CUSHING P.H. (1958). The effect of grazing in reducing the primary production: a review. *Rapp. Cons. Explor. Mer.* **144**, 149–154.

CZARNECKI Z. & FOKSOWICZ T. (1954). Obserwacje dotyczace skladu pokarmu myszolowa zwyczajnego (*Buteo buteo* L.) [Observation on the composition of the feed of buzzard (*Buteo buteo* L.)] *Ekol. Pol.* **2**, 477–484. (In Polish with Russian and English summaries.)

DAVIES P.S. (1966). A constant pressure respirometer for medium sized animals. *Oikos* **17**, 108–112.

DAVIES P.W. & BRINK F. (1942). Microelectrodes for measuring local oxygen tension in animal tissues. *Rev. Sci. Inst.,* **13**, 542–533.

DEEVEY E.S. JR. (1947). Life tables for natural populations of animals. *Quart. Rev. Biol.* **22**, 283–314.

DENMEAD O.T. & BAILEY S.W. (1966). The effects of temperature rise and oxygen depletion on insect survival in stored grain. *J. Stored Prod. Res.* **2**, 35–44.

DIXON A.F.G. (1966). The effect of population density and nutritive status of the host on the summer reproductive activity of the sycamore aphid, *Drepanosiphum platanoides* (Schr.). *J. Anim. Ecol.* **35**, 105–112.

DIXON M. (1937). *Manometric Methods* (1st edn.). Cambridge. (3rd edn. 1951.)

DOBSON R.M. (1962). Marking techniques and their application to the study of small animals. In: *Progress in Soil Zoology,* ed. P.W. Murphy. Butterworth, London, pp. 228–239.

DOWDESWELL W.H. (1959). *Practical Animal Ecology*. Methuen, London.

DOWDESWELL W.H., FISHER R.A. & FORD E.B. (1940) The quantitative study of a population in the Lepidoptera. I. *Polyommatus icaris Rott. Ann. Eugen. Lond.,* 10, 123–136.

DROŻDŻ A. (1965). Wplyw paszy na dojrzewanie plciowe samców nornicy rudej (*Clethrionomys glareolus* Schr.). *Zwierzeta lab.* 3, 34–45.

DROŻDŻ A. (1967). Food preference, food digestibility and natural food supply of small rodents. In: *Secondary Productivity of Terrestrial Ecosystems (Principles and Methods)*. ed. K. Petrusewicz. Warszawa-Kraków. pp. 323–330.

DROŻDŻ A. (1968). Digestibility and utilization of natural foods in small rodents. *Small Mammal Newsletters* 2, 129–131.

DUCKHAM A.N. (1963). *Agricultural Synthesis: The Farming Year*. London.

EDGAR W. (1968). The ecology of *Lycosa lugubris*. Ph.D. Thesis, Univ. of Glasgow.

EDIN H. (1926). Prosecuted researches by indirect methods based on the principle of a marker substance for the determination of the digestibility of feed. The availability of chromium oxide as a marker substance. *Medd 39 cent. Anst. Törsöksor Jordbr.* Stockholm. 80 pp.

EDMONDSON W. (1960). Reproductive rates of rotifers in natural populations. *Mem. Ist. Ital. Hydrobiol.* 12, 21–77.

EDWARDS C.A. (1962). Springtail damage to bean seedlings. *Plant Path.* 11, 67–68.

ELKAN G.H. & MOORE W.E.C. (1962). A rapid method for measurement of carbon dioxide evolution by soil microorganisms. *Ecology* 43, 775–776.

ELLENBY C. & EVANS D.A. (1956). Body weight surface area and oxygen consumption of *Lygia oceanica* and *Drosophila melanogaster*. *J. exp. Biol.* 33, 134–141.

ELLIOTT J.M. (1967). The food of trout (*Salmo trutta*) in a Dartmoor stream. *J. appl. Ecol.* 4, 59–71.

ELSTER H.J. (1955). Ein Beitrag zur Produktionsbiologie des Zooplanktons. *Verh int. Ver. Limnol.* 12, 404–411.

ENGELMANN M.D. (1961). The role of soil arthropods in the energetics of an old-field community. *Ecol. Monogr.* 31, 221–238.

ENGELMANN M.D. (1966). Energetics, terrestrial field studies and animal productivity. In: *Advances in Ecological Research*, ed. J.B. Cragg. London 1, 73–114.

EVANS D.M. (1968). The effect of changes in nutrition of populations of *Microtus agrestis*. *Small Mammal Newsletters* 2, 132.

EVANS F.C. (1949). A population study of house mice following a period of local abundance *J. Mammal.* 30, 351–363.

FAURE J.C. (1932). The phases of locusts in South Africa. *Bull. Ent. Res.* 23, 293–405.

FINDLAY J.D. (1950). The effects of temperature, humidity, air movement and solar radiation on the behaviour and physiology of cattle and other farm animals. *Hanna Dairy Research Institute. Bulletin* No. 9, 178 pp.

FISHER R.A. & FORD E.B. (1947). The spread of a gene in natural conditions in a colony of the moth *Panaxia dominula* L., *Heredity* 1, 143–174.

FOURCHE J. (1967). La réspiration chez *Drosophila melanogaster* au cours de la métamorphose. Influence de la pupaison, de la mue nymphale et de l'émergence. *J. Insect Physiol.* 13, 1269–1277.

GAJEVSKAYA N.S. (1959). Sur l'étude quantitative de l'alimentation des animaux aquatiques. *Proc. XV Int. Cong. Zool. Lond.* 769–772.

GIBB J.A. & BETTS M.M. (1963). Food and food supply of nestling tits (*Paridae*) in Breckland Pine. *J. Anim. Ecol.* **32**, 489–533.

GLASGOW J.P. (1953). The extermination of animal populations by artificial predation and the estimation of populations. *J. Anim. Ecol.* **22**, 32–46.

GLIWICZ J., ANDRZEJEWSKI R., BUJALSKA G. & PETRUSEWICZ K. (1968). Productivity investigation of an island population of *Clethrionomys glareolus* (Schreber, 1780). I. Dynamics of cohorts. *Acta theriol.* **13**, 401–413.

GLIWICZ Z.M. (1969). The share of algae, bacteria and tripton in the food of the pelagic zooplankton of the various trophy lakes. *Bull. Acad. pol. Sci. Cl.* **II.** 17.

GOLLEY F.B. (1960). Energy dynamics of a food chain of an old-field community. *Ecol. Monogr.* **30**, 187–206.

GOLLEY F.B. (1961). Energy values of ecological materials. *Ecology* **42**, 581–584.

GOLLEY F.B. (1967). Methods of measuring secondary productivity in terrestrial vertebrate populations. In: *Secondary Productivity of Terrestrial Ecosystems (Principles and Methods)*, ed. K. Petrusewicz, Warszawa-Kraków. pp. 99–124.

GOODMAN G.T. (1963). The role of mineral nutrients in *Eriophorum* communities. I. The effects of added ground limestone upon growth in an *Eriophorum augustifolium* community. *J. Ecol.,* **51**, 205–220.

GÓRECKI A. (1967). Caloric value of the body in small rodents. In: *Secondary Productivity of Terrestrial Ecosystems (Principles and Methods)*, ed. K. Petrusewicz, Warszawa-Kraków. pp. 315–321.

GÓRECKI A. & GRODZIŃSKI W. (1968). Metabolic rate and energy budgets of some voles and mice. *Small Mammal Newsletters* **2**, 132–137.

GRAINGER J.N.R. (1956). Effects of changes of temperature on the respiration of certain Crustacea. *Nature* **178**, 930–931.

GRAINGER J.N.R. (1958). First stages in the adaptation of poikilotherms to temperature change. In: Carlson, L.D. (ed.). *Federation Proceedings of the American Physiological Society,* **17**, 1044–1073.

GREEN C.D. (1964). The effect of crowding upon the fecundity of *Folsomia candida* (William) var. *distincta* (Bagnall) (*Collembola*). *Ent. exp. appl.* Amsterdam. 62–70.

GREGG J.H. & LINTS F.A. (1967). A constant-volume respirometer for *Drosophila* imagos. *C.R. Lab. Carlsberg* **36**, 25–34.

GRODZIŃSKI W., BOBEK B., DROŻDŻ A. & GÓRECKI A. (1968). Energy flow through small rodents in a beech forest. *Small Mammal Newsletters* **2**, 146–150.

GRODZIŃSKI W., PUCEK Z. & RYSZKOWSKI L. (1966). Estimation of rodent numbers by means of prebaiting and intensive removal. *Acta theriol.* **11**, 297–314.

GRÜM L. (1969). Analiza przestrzennego zróżnicowania w ruchliwości biegaczowatych (*Carabidae, Coleoptera*) [Analysis of spatial diversity in mobility of ground-beetles (*Carabidae, Coleoptera*)]. *Ekol. Pol. A.*

HAAHN F. (1965). Designing for physiological data. *BioScience* (American Institute of Biological Sciences) **15**, 112–115.

HAIRSTON N.G. & BYERS G.W. (1954). A study in community ecology: the soil arthropods in a field in southern Michigan. *Contr. Lab. Vert. Biol. Univ. Mich.* **64**, 1–37.

HARTLEY P.T.H. (1948). Food and feeding relationships in a community of freshwater fishes. *J. Anim. Ecol.* **17**, 1–14.

HARTLEY P.T.H. (1953). An ecological study of the feeding habits of the English titmice. *J. Anim. Ecol.* **22**, 261–288.

HAWKINS A.C. (1958). A self-adjusting unit for the control of an animal calorimeter. *J. sci. Instrum.* **35**, 440–443.

HAYNE D.W. (1949). Calculation of size of home-range. *J. Mammal.* **30**, 1–18.

HEALEY I.N. (1965). Studies on the production biology of soil *Collembola,* with special reference to a species of *Onychiurus.* Thesis: D.Ph. University College of Swansea. 198 pp.

HEALEY I.N. (1967). The energy flow through population of soil Collembola. In: *Secondary Productivity of Terrestrial Ecosystems (Principles and Methods),* ed. K. Petrusewicz. Warszawa-Kraków. pp. 695–708.

HILLBRICHT-ILKOWSKA A. (1967). Attempt of the evaluation of the production and turnover of plankton rotifers on the example of *Keratella cochlearis* (Gosse). *Bull. Acad. pol. Sci. Cl. II,* **15**, 35–40.

HOLTER H. (1943). Technique of the cartesian diver. *C.R. Lab. Carlsberg* (Sér. Chim.) **24**, 400–478.

HORTON P.A. (1961). Bionomics of brown trout in a Dartmoor stream. *J. Anim. Ecol.* **30**, 311–338.

HUGHES R.N. (1968). The population ecology and energetics of *Scrobicularia plana.* Ph.D. Thesis, University of Wales, Bangor.

HUNTER R.F. (1958). Hill sheep and their pasture—a study of sheep grazing in S.E. Scotland. *J. Ecol.* **50**, 651.

ITO T. & FRAENKEL G. (1966). The effects of nitrogen starvation on *Tenebrio molitor* L. *J. Insect Physiol.* **12**, 893–807.

IVLEV V.G. (1934). Eine Mikromethode zur Bestimmung des Kaloriengehalts von Nahrstoffen. *Biochem. Z.* **275**, 49–55.

IVLEV V.G. (1945). Biologičeskaja produktivnost' vodoemov. *Usp. sovr. Biol.* **19**, 98–120.

JACKSON C.H.N. (1939). The analysis of an animal population. *J. Anim. Ecol.* **8**, 238–246.

JACKSON C.H.N. (1948). The analysis of a tsetse fly population. III. *Ann. Eugen. Lond.* **14**, 91–108.

JAMES D.B. (1964). Locating earthquake survivors. *Ion Exchange Progress* **3**, 1–4.

JAMES W.O. & JAMES A.L. (1940). The respiration of barley germinating in the dark. *New Phytol.* **39**, 145–176.

JENKINS D., WATSON A. & MILLER G.R. (1963). Population studies on red grouse, *Lagopus lagopus scoticus* (Lath.) in north-east Scotland. *J. Anim. Ecol.* **32**, 317–376.

JENSEN C.R. VAN, GUNDY S.D. & STOLZY L.H. (1966). Diffusion-exchange respirometer using the CO_2 electrode. *Nature* **211**, 608–610.

JOLLY G.M. (1965). Explicit estimates from capture-recapture data with both death and immigration; Stochastic model. *Biometrika,* **52**, 225.

JØRGENSEN N.R. (1916). Untersøgelser over Frequensflader og korrelation. Copenhagen.

JUDAY C. (1940). The annual energy budget of an inland lake. *Ecology* **21**, 438–450.

JUDAY C. & SCHOMER H.A. (1935). The utilisation of solar radiation by algae at different depth in lakes. *Biol. Bull.* **69**, 75–81.

KAJAK A. (1967). Productivity of some populations of web spiders. In: *Secondary Productivity of Terresterial Ecosystems (Principles and Methods)*, ed. K. Petrusewicz. Warszawa-Kraków. pp. 807–820.

KAWANABE H. (1958). On the significance of the social structure for the mode of density effect in a salmon-like fish "Ayu" *Plecoglassus altivelis* Temminck et Schlegel. *Mem. Coll. Sci. Univ. Kyoto (Ser.* 13) **25**, 171–180.

KAWANABE H. (1959). Food competition among fishes in some rivers of Kyoto prefecture, Japan. *Mem. Coll. Sci. Univ. Kyoto (Ser.* 13) **26**, 253–268.

KLEIBER M. (1961). *The Fire of Life: an Introduction to Animal Energetics.* Wiley, New York. 454 pp.

KLEKOWSKI R.Z., PRUS T. & ŻYROMSKA-RUDZKA H. (1967). Elements of energy budget of *Tribolium castaneum* (Hbst) in its developmental cycle. In: *Secondary Productivity of Terrestrial Ecosystems (Principles and Methods)*, ed. K. Petrusewicz. Warszawa-Kraków. pp. 859–879.

KLUIJVER H.N. (1933). Contribution to the biology and the ecology of the starling (*Sturnus vulgaris vulgaris* L.) during its reproductive period. *Versl. PlZiekt. Dienst Wageningen* **69**, 1–145.

KO W.E.Y. (1965). Progress in miniaturized biotelemetry. *BioScience (A.I.B.S.)* **15**, 118–120.

KO W.E.Y. & THOMPSON W. (1963). The tunnel diode in biotelemetry. *Medical Electronics and Biological Engineering* **1**, 363–369.

KOMOR J. (1940). Über die Ausnützung des Sonnenlichtes beim Wachstum der grünen Pflanzen. *Biochem. Z.* **305**, 381–395.

KÖPF H. (1952). Laufende Messungen der Bodenatmung im Freiland. *Landw. Forsch.* **4**, 186–194.

KROGH A. (1914). The quantitative relation between temperature and standard metabolism in animals. *Int. Z. phys.-chem. Biol.* **1**, 491–508.

KROGH A. (1940). A microclimatic recorder. *Ecology* **21**, 275–279.

KOZLOVSKY D.C. (1968). A critical evaluation of the trophic level concept. 1. Ecological efficiencies. *Ecology* **49**, 48–60.

LACK D. (1966). *Population studies of Birds.* Oxford. 341 pp.

LAMB K.P. (1961). Some effects of fluctuating temperatures on metabolism development and rate of population growth in the cabbage aphid, *Brevicoryne brassicae. Ecology* **42**, 740–745.

LANGLEY P.A. (1967). The control of digestion in the tsetse fly, *Glossina morsitans:* A comparison between field flies and flies reared in captivity. *J. Insect Physiol.* **13**, 477–486.

LAVOISIER A.L. (1780). Mémoire sur la chaleur. *Mémoires de l'académie Royal.* 355 pp.

LE FEBVRE E.A. (1964). The use of $D_2{}^{18}O$ for measuring energy metabolism in *Columba livia* at rest and in flight. *Auk* **81**, 403–416.

LESLIE P.H. (1952). The estimation of population parameters from data obtained by means of the capture-recapture method. II. The estimation of total numbers. *Biometrika* **38**, 269–292.

LIFSON N., GORDON G.B. & McCLINTOCK R. (1955). Measurement of total carbon dioxide production by means of $D_2{}^{18}O$. *J. appl. Physiol.* **7**, 704–710.

LINDEMANN R.L. (1942). The trophic-dynamic aspect of ecology. *Ecology* **23**, 399–418.

LINDERSTRØM-LANG K. (1943). On the theory of the Cartesian diver microrespirometer. *C.R. Lab. Carlsberg (Ser. Chim.)* **24**, 333–398.

LINTS C.V., LINTS F.A. & ZEUTHEN E. (1967): Respiration in *Drosophila*. 1. Oxygen consumption during development of the egg in genotypes of *Drosophila melanogaster* with contributions to the gradient diver technique. *C.R. Lab. Carlsberg* **36**, 35–66.

LØVILLE A. & ZEUTHEN E. (1962). The gradient diver, a recording instrument for gasometric micro-analysis. *C.R. Lab. Carlsberg* **32**, 513–534.

LOVTRUP S. & LARSSON S. (1965). Electromagnetic recording diver balance. *Nature* **208**, 1116–1117.

MACFADYEN A. (1948). The meaning of productivity in biological systems. *J. Anim. Ecol.* **17**, 75–80.

MACFADYEN A. (1961). A new system for continuous respirometry of small air-breathing invertebrates in near-natural conditions. *J. exp. Biol.* **38**, 323–341.

MACFADYEN A. (1963a). *Animal Ecology: Aims and Methods*. London. 344 pp.

MACFADYEN A. (1963b). The contributions of the microfauna to total soil metabolism. In: *Soil organisms*, ed. J. Doeksen & J. van der Drift. Amsterdam. pp. 1–17.

MACFADYEN A. (1964). Energy flow in ecosystems and its exploitation by grazing. In: *Grazing in Terrestrial and Marine Environments*, ed. D.J. Crisp. Blackwell, Oxford. pp. 3–20.

MACFADYEN A. (1967). Methods of investigation of productivity of invertebrates in terrestrial ecosystems. In: *Secondary Productivity of Terrestrial Ecosystems* (*Principles and Methods*), ed. K. Petrusewicz. Warszawa-Kraków. pp. 383–412.

MACFADYEN A. (1968). The measurement of climate in studies of soil and litter animals. In: *The Measurement of Environmental Factors in Terrestrial Ecology*, ed. E.M. Wadsworth. Blackwell, Oxford, pp. 59–68.

MACFADYEN A. (in prep.). The inhibitory effect of carbon dioxide on metabolism of certain soils.

MACKAY R.S. (1968). *Bio-medical Telemetry: Sensing and Transmitting Biological Information from Animals and Man*. Wiley. 388 pp.

MALČEVSKIJ A.S. & KADOČNIKOV N.P. (1953). Metodika prižiznennogo izučenija pitanija ptencov nasekomojadnych ptic. *Zool. Z.* **32**, 277–282.

MARTIN D.J. (1964). Analysis of sheep diet. In: *Grazing in Terrestrial and Marine Environments*, ed. D.J. Crisp. Blackwell, Oxford. pp. 173–188.

McGREGOR K.A. (1968). *Productivity relations between insects and oak trees*. D.Ph. Thesis, University of Oxford.

MESSENGER P.S. (1964). Use of life tables in a bioclimatic study of an experimental aphid-braconid wasp host-parasite system. *Ecology* **45**, 119–131.

MILES P.M. (1947). An introduction to the study of *Collembola*. *Proc. S. Lond. Ent. Nat. Hist. Soc.* (1946–1947) 85–102.

MILLER R.S. (1954). Food habits of the wood-mouse, *Apodemus sylvaticus* (Linné, 1758), and the bank vole, *Clethrionomys glareolus* (Schreber, 1780) in Wytham Woods, Berkshire. *Saügetierk. Mitt.* **11**, 109–114.

MILNER C. (1967). The estimation of energy flow through populations of large herbivorous mammals. In: *Secondary Productivity of Terrestrial Ecosystems* (*Principles and Methods*), ed. K. Petrusewicz. Warszawa-Kraków. pp. 147–161.

MITTLER T.E. (1967). Effect on aphid feeding of dietary methionine. *Nature* **214**, 386.

MØLLER C.M., MÜLLER D. & NIELSEN J. (1954a). Ein Diagramm der Stoffproduktion im Buchenwald. *Berichte der Schweizerischen Botanischen Gesellschaft* **64**, 487–494.

MØLLER C.M., MÜLLER D. & NIELSEN J. (1954b). Graphic presentation of dry matter production of European Beech. *Det Forstlige Forsøgsvaesen* **21**, 327–335.

MÜLLER D. & NIELSEN J. (1965). Production brute, pertes par réspiration et production nette dans la foret ombrophile tropicale. *Det Forstlige Forsøgsvaesen* **29**, 69–160.

NAUMOV N.P. (1963). *Ekologija životnych.* Moscow. 617 pp.

NEESS J. & DUGDALE R.C. (1959). Computation of production for populations of aquatic midge larvae. *Ecology* **40**, 425–430.

NEWELL R.C. (1966). The effect of temperature on the metabolism of poikilotherms. *Nature* **212**, 426–428.

NIELSEN C.O. (1949). Studies on the soil microfauna. II. The soil-inhabiting nematodes. *Natura Jutlandica* **2**, 1–131.

NIELSON C.O. (1961). Respiratory metabolism of some populations of enchytraeid worms and free living nematodes. *Oikos* **12**, 17–35.

NIELSEN E., TETENS & EVANS D.G. (1960). Duration of the pupal stage of *Aedes taeniorhynchus* with a discussion of the velocity of development as a function of temperature. *Oikos* **11**, 200–222.

OATLEY C.W. (1966). The scanning electron microscope: a new British instrument. *Spectrum,* London. 3 pp.

ODUM E.P. (1959). *Fundamentals of Ecology.* Philadelphia and London. 546 pp.

ODUM E.P. (1960). Organic production and turnover in old field succession. *Ecology* **41**, 34–49.

ODUM E.P., CONNELL, C.E. & STODDARD H.L. (1961). Flight energy and estimated flight ranges of some migrating birds. *Auk* **78**, 515–527.

ODUM E.P., MARSHALL S.G. & MARPLES T.G. (1965). The calorific content of migrating birds. *Ecology* **46**, 901–904.

ODUM E.P. & GOLLEY F.B. (1963). Radioactive tracers as an aid to the measurement of energy flow at the population level in nature. In: *Radioecology,* ed. V. Schultz & A.W. Klement. New York. pp. 403–410.

O'HARA J. (1968). The influence of weight and temperature in the metabolic rate of sunfish. *Ecology* **49**, 159–161.

PARIS O.H. & SIKORA A. (1967). Radiotracer analysis of the trophic dynamics of natural isopod populations. In: *Secondary Productivity of Terrestrial Ecosystems (Principles and Methods),* ed. K. Petrusewicz. Warszawa-Kraków. pp. 741–771.

PARR M.J., GASKELL T.J. & GEORGE B.J. (1968). Capture-recapture methods of estimating animal numbers, *J. Biol. Educ.* **2**, 95–117.

PEČEN G.A. (1965). Produkcija vetvistousych rakoobraznych ozernogo zooplanktona. *Gidrobiol. Z.* **1**, 19–26.

PETRUSEWICZ K. (1963). Population growth induced by disturbance in ecological structure of the population. *Ekol. Pol.* **11**, 87–125.

PETRUSEWICZ K. (1966). Production vs. turnover of biomass and individuals. *Bull. Acad. pol. Sci. Cl. II,* **9**, 621–625.

PETRUSEWICZ K. (1967a). Concepts in studies on the secondary productivity of terrestrial ecosystems. In: *Secondary Productivity of Terrestrial Ecosystems* (*Principles and Methods*), ed. K. Petrusewicz. Warszawa-Kraków. pp. 17–49.

PETRUSEWICZ K. (1967b). Suggested list of more important concepts in productivity studies (definitions and symbols). In: *Secondary Productivity of Terrestrial Ecosystems* (*Principles and Methods*), ed. K. Petrusewicz. Warszawa-Kraków. pp. 51–58.

PETRUSEWICZ K. & ANDRZEJEWSKI R. (1962). Natural history of a free-living population of house mice (*Mus musculus* L.), with particular reference to grouping within the population. *Ekol. Pol. A*, **10**, 85–122.

PETRUSEWICZ K., ANDRZEJEWSKI R., BUJALSKA G. & GLIWICZ J. (1968). Productivity investigation of an island population of *Clethrionomys glareolus* (Schreber, 1780). IV. Production. *Acta theriol.* **13**, 435–455.

PHILLIPSON J. (1960). A contribution to the feeding biology of *Mitopus morio* (F.) (*Phalangiida*). *J. Anim. Ecol.* **29**, 35–43.

PHILLIPSON J. (1962). Respirometry and the study of energy turnover in natural systems with particular reference to harvest spiders (*Phalangiida*). *Oikos* **13**, 311–318.

PHILLIPSON J. (1963). The use of respiratory data in estimating annual respiratory metabolism, with particular reference to *Leiobunum rotundum* (Latr.) (*Phalangiida*). *Oikos* **14**, 212–223.

PHILLIPSON J. (1964). A miniature bomb calorimeter for small biological samples. *Oikos* **15**, 130–139.

PHILLIPSON J. (1967a). Secondary productivity in invertebrates reproducing more than once in a lifetime. In: *Secondary Productivity of Terrestrial Ecosystems* (*Principles and Methods*), ed. K. Petrusewicz. Warszawa-Kraków. pp. 459–475.

PHILLIPSON J. (1967b). Studies on the bioenergetics of woodland *Diplopoda*. In: *Secondary Productivity of Terrestrial Ecosystems* (*Principles and Methods*), ed. K. Petrusewicz. Warszawa-Kraków. pp. 679–683.

PILARSKA J. (*in litt.*). Individual growth curve and consumption of hare (*Lepus europaeus Pall.*).

RAW F. (1960). Earthworm population studies; a comparison of sampling methods. *Nature, London* **187**, 257.

REICHLE D.E. (1967). Radioisotope turnover and energy flow in terrestrial isopod populations, *Ecology* **48**, 351–366.

RICKER W.E. (1946). Production and utilization of fish populations. *Ecol. Monogr.* **6**, 373–391.

SATCHELL J. (1955). An electrical method of sampling earthworm populations. *Soil Zoology*, ed. D.K.McE. Kevan. Butterworth, London. 356–364. 1962.

SCHOLANDER P.F. (1942). Volumetric microrespirometers. *Rev. Sci. Instrum.* **13**, 32–33.

SCHOLANDER P.F. (1950). Volumetric plastic respirometer. *Rev. Sci. Instrum.* **21**, 378–380.

SCHOLANDER P.F., DAM L. VAN & KANWISHER J.W. (1955). Microgasometric determination of dissolved oxygen and nitrogen. *Bull. Biol.* **109**, 328–334.

SHORT H.L. & REMMENGA E.E. (1965). Use of fecal cellulose to estimate plant tissue eaten by deer. *J. Range Mgt.* **18**, 139–144.

SIMPSON G.G., ROE A. & LEWONTIN R.C. (1960). *Quantitative zoology*. New York. 440 pp.

SLOBODKIN L.B. (1954). Population dynamics in *Daphnia obtusa* Kurz. *Ecol. Monogr.* **24**, 69–88.

SLOBODKIN L.B. (1959). Energetics in *Daphnia pulex* populations. *Ecology* **40**, 232–243.

SLOBODKIN L.B. (1960). Ecological energy relationships at the population level. *Amer. Nat.* **94**, 213–236.

SLOBODKIN L.B. & RICHMAN S. (1961). Calories per gram in species of animals. *Nature London* **191**, 299.

Soo Hoo C.F. & FRAENKEL G. (1966a). The selection of food plants in a polyphagous insect, *Prodenia eridania* (Cramer). *J. Insect Physiol.* **12**, 693–709.

Soo Hoo C.F. & FRAENKEL G. (1966b). The consumption, digestion and utilization of food plants by a polyphagous insect, *Prodenia eridania* (Cramer). *J. Insect Physiol.* **12**, 711–730.

SOUTHERN H.N. (1954). Tawny owls and their prey. *Ibis* **96**, 384–410.

SOUTHWICK C.H. (1955). Regulatory mechanisms of house mouse population: social behaviour affecting litter survival. *Ecology* **36**, 627–634.

SOUTHWOOD T.R.E. (1966). *Ecological methods*. Methuen, London.

STEWARD D.R.M. (1967). Analysis of plant epidermis in faeces: a technique for studying the food preferences of grazing herbivores. *J. appl. Ecol.* **4**, 83–111.

SWABY R.J. & PASSEY B.I. (1953). A simple macrorespirometer for studies in soil microbiology. *Aust. J. agric. Res.* **4**, 334–339.

SWIETOSLAWSKI W. (1946). *Microcalorimetry*. Reinhold, New York.

TANNER C.B., THURTELL G.T. & SWANN J.B. (1963). Integration systems using a commercial coulombmeter. *Soil Sci. Soc. Amer. Proc.* **27**, 478–481.

TANTON M.T. (1965). Problems of live-trapping and population estimation for the wood mouse, *Apodemus sylvaticus* (L.). *J. Anim. Ecol.* **34**, 1–22.

TEAL J.M. (1957). Community metabolism in a temperate cold spring. *Ecol. Monogr.* **27**, 283–302.

THORSON G. (1950). Reproductive and larval ecology of marine bottom invertebrates. *Biol. Rev.* **25**, 1–45.

TOBIAS J.M. (1943). Microrespiration techniques. *Physiol. Rev.* **23**, 51–75.

TROJAN P. (1968). Ecological model of maintenance costs in *Microtus arvalis* (Pall.). *Small Mammal Newsletters* **2**, 80–182.

UMBREIT W.W., BURRIS R.H. & STAUFFER J.F. (1957). *Manometric techniques* (3rd edn.). Minneapolis, Burgess. 338 pp.

VAN DYNE G.M. & MEYER J.H. (1964). A method for measurement of forage intake of grazing livestock using microinjection techniques. *J. Range Mgt.* **17**, 204–208.

VARLEY G.C. (1967). The effects of grazing by animals on plant productivity. In: *Secondary Productivity of Terrestrial Ecosystems* (*Principles and Methods*), ed. K. Petrusewicz Warszawa-Kraków. pp. 773–776.

WAGER H.G. & PORTER F.A.E. (1961). An apparatus for the automatic measurement of oxygen uptake by electrolytic replacement of the oxygen consumed. *Biochem. J.* **81**, 614–616.

WALKOWA W. & PETRUSEWICZ K. (1967). Net production of confined mouse populations. In: *Secondary Productivity of Terrestrial Ecosystems* (*Principles and Methods*), ed. K Petrusewicz. Warszawa-Kraków. pp. 335–347.

WALLWORK J.A. (1958). Notes on the feeding behaviour of some forest soil *Acarina*. *Oikos* **9**, 260–271.

WEBB N. (1968) *Comparative studies on population metabolism in soil arthropods*. 100 pp Ph.D. Thesis, University of Wales, Swansea.

WELLINGTON W.G. (1960). Qualitative changes in natural populations during change in abundance. *Canad. J. Zool.* **38**, 289–314.

WELTY J.C. (1962). *The life of birds*. Philadelphia and London. 546 pp.

WESTLAKE D.F. (1963). Comparisons of plant productivity. *Biol. Rev.* **38**, 385–425.

WIEGERT R.G. (1964). Population energetics of meadow spittlebugs (*Philaenus spumarius* L.) as affected by migration and habitat. *Ecol. Monogr.* **34**, 225–241.

WIEGERT R.G. (1965). Energy dynamics of the grasshopper populations in old field and alfalfa field ecosystems. *Oikos* **16**, 161–176.

WIEGERT R.G. & EVANS F.C. (1967). Investigations of secondary productivity in grasslands. In: *Secondary Productivity of Terrestrial Ecosystems (Principles and Methods)*, ed. K. Petrusewicz. Warszawa-Kraków. pp. 499–518.

WIERZBOWSKA T. & PETRUSEWICZ K. (1963). Residency and rate of disappearance of two free-living populations of the house mouse (*Mus musculus* L.). *Ekol. Pol. A.* **11**, 557–574.

WIESER W. (1962). Parameter des Sauerstoffverbrauches. I. Der Sauerstoffverbrauch einiger Landisopoden. *Z. vergl. Physiol.* **45**, 247–271.

WIGGLESWORTH V.B. (1935). Respiration in the flea *Xenopsylla*. *Proc. Roy. Soc. B.* **118**, 397–419.

WIGGLESWORTH V.B. (1939) (and later editions). *The Principles of Insect Physiology* Methuen (4th edn. 1950). 544 pp.

WILLIAMS E.C. JR. & REICHLE D.E. (1968). Radioactive tracers in the study of energy turnover by a grazing insect (*Chrysochus auratus* Fab.). *Oikos* **19**, 10–18.

WILLIAMS G. (1962). Seasonal and diurnal activity of harvestmen (*Phalangiida*) and spiders (*Araneida*) in contrasted habitats. *J. Anim. Ecol.* **31**, 23–42.

WINBERG G.G. (1934). Opyt izučenija fotosinteza i dychanija v vodnoj masse ozera. K voprosu o balanse organičeskogo veščestva. Soobšč. 1. Trudy limnol. *St. v Kosine* **18**, 5–24.

WINBERG G.G. (1936). Nekotorye obščie voprosy produktivnosti ozer. *Zool. Z.* **15**, 587–603.

WINBERG G.G. (1960). *Pervičnaja Produkcija Vodoemov*. Minsk. 329 pp.

WINBERG G.G. (1966). Skorost' rosta i intensivnost' obmena u životnych. *Usp. sovrem. Biol.* **61**, 274–293.

WINBERG G.G. (editor) (1968). *Metody opredelenija produkcii vodnych zivotnych*. (*The Methods for the Estimation of Production of Aquatic Animals*.) Minsk. 242 pp.

WINBERG G.G., PEČEN' T.A. & ŠUŠKINA E.A. (1965). Produkcija planktonnych rakoobraznych v trech ozerach raznogo tipa. *Zool. Z.* **49**, 676–687.

WINTERINGHAM F.P.W. (1959). An electrolytic respirometer for insects. *Laboratory Practice* **8**, 372–375.

ZEJDA J. (1966). Litter size in *Clethrionomys glareolus* Schreber 1780. *Zool. Listy* **15**, 193–206.

ZEUTHEN E. (1947). Body size and metabolic rate in the animal kingdom. *C.R. Lab. Carlsberg (Sér. Chim.)* **26**, 17–165.
ZEUTHEN E. (1950). Cartesian diver respirometer. *Biol. Bull.* **98**, 139–143.
ZEUTHEN E. (1964). *Microgasometric Methods: Cartesian Divers.* Second Intern. Cong. Histo- and Cytochemistry, Springer, Frankfurt am Main. 70-80.

Index

Index